No More Bings In Benarty

an account of the rise and fall of
coal mining in the Benarty Area of
Fife, and its influence on the lives
of the people who lived there.

Produced by BENARTY MINING HERITAGE GROUP
Collated and Edited by Les Cooney & Alex Maxwell

Acknowledgements

Benarty Mining Heritage Group would like to thank the following organisations whose assistance, financial and otherwise, made this publication possible:-

Fife Regional Council

Dunfermline District Council

Lochore Miners Social Club

Ballingry Community Council

Ballingry Village Hall Management Committee

Ballingry Community Centre Management Committee and staff

S.M. Bayne and Company

Lauder College — Community Studies Staff

We are also indebted to the Dunfermline Press for allowing us the use of extracts from their newspapers of former days, and to Eddie Henderson for information from his book "History of Lochoreshire".

In addition to the above there were numerous other people who contributed newspaper cuttings, photographs and personal stories of the past and to all of them we express our thanks.

On the cover: Pulley Wheel, A. McGachie and Children.

Price: £4.00

ISBN 0 9520674 0 4

Contents

To The Readers

This book is not claiming to be the last word on the Mining Heritage of Benarty.

It is in essence a compilation of historical fact and personal recollections of people who have spent their lives in this Area and no doubt there will be controversy and debate amongst those who read it, about some of the events and characters described.

Neither of course do we claim to be professional writers, although we think you will find the book quite readable and enjoyable.

Actually, we do hope it does generate discussion and debate, reminding us of all our Mining Heritage, and perhaps stimulating others to take up their pens as well.

And for that we offer no apology!

Benarty Mining Heritage Group.

INTRODUCTION

To the casual visitor travelling from Lochgelly towards Ballingry, there are few obvious signs along the way that what they see from a distance are other than a sequence of rural villages, nestling in a valley in the shadow of Benarty Hill. The quiet, the green fields, the waters of the Lochore Meadows Country Park, the slopes of the Ochil Hills in the distance on one side, and the Lomond Hills on the other contribute to a picturesque view, which almost justifies the description by some of the older residents as 'the most beautiful place in the world', although they will also tell you that people from the East of Fife have described it in less flattering terms. Nevertheless it is attractive.

The first hint that this tranquillity disguises a more murky past is a lone, isolated building which has seen better days, with no apparent reason for being there, except a sign which reads 'Glencraig Miners Club'. You look in vain for the Colliery.

Further along the road, at the entrance to 'The Meadows' rests a symbolic pulley wheel, and in the distance beyond the trim golf course, a pit-head frame stands out starkly against the skyline, a striking reminder of a byegone day.

And then you come to an impressive large building at a road junction, which is identified by a notice 'Lochore Miners Social Club', obviously a thriving establishment — and the Tower Clock is working!

These sights are the confirmation that your first impressions were deceptive.

For this tranquillity was not always so. This pleasant countryside was once a busy coal-mining area, the land despoiled by pit bings, the people's lives centred around, and dominated by, the coal industry, and the quality of those living dependent on its fluctuating fortunes over more than a century.

The younger generation today may know little of their Mining Heritage, of what shaped their lives and gave these villages their reason for being, but if they wish to understand the present, they have to appreciate the past.

Because it was the discovery of coal in this area, and the rise and fall in demand for that coal, over more than a century, which shaped not just the working lives of those who lived in these mining villages, but also fashioned their particular social, cultural and political features as well. The Coal Industry gave these villages their specific identity. It is the single thread which linked together all the events and characters of this area and allows us to understand them.

Their Mining Heritage is one of boom and slump, of struggle, strikes and conflict, of relative prosperity and poverty in turn, relieved often only by an intense Community spirit, which is peculiar and common to Mining areas. The very nature of their work bound them together as nothing else could. Underground each depended on his neighbour to survive, and that bond remained in the Communities above.

I believe that this Mining Heritage is of tremendous importance, and that the young people in these villages should understand and appreciate it, because it is dying away. That was why I welcomed the initiative of those older citizens who came together to examine history, to recollect and share their own life's experiences, and to tell their tales of days gone by, so that we can all benefit from their collective efforts.

This book is the product of that effort, a mixture of fact, memories and personal stories. I am sure that anyone who has any interest at all in local history will welcome their efforts and I am pleased to have been associated with them.

Councillor Alex Maxwell J.P.

CHAPTER 1

From Monks to the Mary

As a natural source of fuel and energy, coal has played a significant role in the history and economy of Scotland. It has been sought after and mined in one form or another since Roman times at least, although the earliest recorded evidence of coal-mining does not appear until the early part of the twelfth century, when it seems, the monks of Newbattle Abbey were excavating outcrops along the Esk Valley.

Elsewhere, certainly in many parts of Central Scotland, coal was being used for local requirements, primarily for evaporating sea water to extract the much needed and highly prized salt. As a domestic fuel it had its limitations, however, and the record books state that an Act of Parliament was passed in 1306 forbidding the burning of coal in London, as it was becoming a major pollution problem!

In Fife, as in the rest of the country, it seems that the first real coal gatherers came from the ranks of the clergy, and in the 13th century, the monks of Dunfermline were given the right to dig for coal in the lands of Pittencrieff. This, one of the oldest charters in Scotland, was given to the Abbot and Convent of Dunfermline by one William de Oberwill, the holder of the Pittencrieff Estates, and it allowed the good friars to work one pit on the lands. Once this pit had been exhausted, the monks had the right to seek out and dig another one, but the charter stipulated that any coal recovered must be for the sole use of the Abbey and the monks were expressly forbidden to sell any of it.

They could, however, give the coal to local people in the form of alms.

On a pilgrimage to Dunfermline during the reign of King James II, Aeneas Silvious, the poet and scholar who would later become Pope Pius II, witnessed the monks at the Abbey distributing 'black stones', which as Silvious explained, were "impregnated with inflammable substances" and the people would take them home to burn as a substitute for wood.

By the beginning of the 16th century some progress had been made in the mining processes, but it was still a highly hazardous procedure. The problems involved in draining the coal pits, for instance, meant that mining below levels greater than 30 metres, was well nigh impossible. Excavations, therefore, were more or less restricted to outcrops and shallow 'bell' pits, neither of which yielded more than a few tonnes at a time. When one pit was cleared another had to be sought out and dug, and the whole process would begin again. A time consuming affair that provided little more than the most basic of needs. Little wonder then, that the industry was seldom seen as being important to the local community.

However, about this time, advances were being made and output began to rise slowly but surely. Horses were now being used in the haulage from the coal face to the pit surface as well as in the transportation of the coal.

Drainage still presented problems and outcrop coal, which could be gathered from the shore or on the banks of the local streams still formed the bulk of the 'crop'. In the deeper mines, shallow pits or 'sinks' had to be inserted at intervals along the coal seam to supply fresh air to the workings.

Once these workings had been sunk to below the level of the mine, the entire pit had either to be abandoned or else a 'Dam and Wave' system had to be employed. This was an extremely laborious task. At the point where the dip began, a clay dam had to be built and the water that had gathered there had to be bailed out by hand. The method was both time-consuming and wasteful, and coal became in short supply, so much so that in the reign of Mary, Queen of Scots, Parliament passed an Act forbidding the export of the fuel. As demand increased, the search for coal seams within Fife became more and more widespread.

By 1560 coal mining was already a going concern in the Benarty area and the Barony of Inchgall recorded in its characters the production of coal, along with limestone, peat and 'divots' as being among its appendages. Coal was also being mined at Crosshill and Blair, as well as other parts of Fife and was increasingly being used in the 'Salt-Pan' and metal industries. Production steadily increased from an estimated 40,000 tonnes nationally in the 1550s to well over half a million tonnes in 1707. Most of this came from the coalfields of Fife and the Lothians.

Mining had begun to establish itself as the main industry of the villages and communities in the Benarty district, employing many women and children as well as the menfolk in the production processes. At Blair, for example, in 1715, women and children were used to haul the coal to the surface thus allowing the face workers to concentrate on digging.

The invention of the steam engine by James Watt changed the industry beyond all recognition in the middle of the 18th century as power now became available to raise men, materials and coal from greater depths than ever thought possible. Now depths of 300 metres and more could be reached during the next hundred years or so. Output increased to a staggering 17 million tonnes as the demands of the ever-expanding heavy industries were met.

From 1835 onwards, coal mining began to establish itself as one of the major industries in the Benarty area, and new, larger Mining Companies came into being.

Two local land-owning families, the Goodalls of Bowhill, who currently held the lease to the Cluny Colliery from the Raith Estate, and the Aytoun family, owners of the Capledrae Estate, joined forces to create the Capledrae Cannel Coal Company, with Thomas Goodall as its first manager.

The new Company sunk two pits in the district, 'Manorlees', which lay just south of Kirkness House and 'Flockhouse', on land near Capledrae Farm. Eventually a third pit, 'The Squirrel', would be opened at Westerfield.

Houses were built at Westfield and Flockhouse to accommodate the Company's growing workforce, and gradually, this once largely uninhabited area, began to take on the appearance of an industrial 'boom town', as more and more workers were brought in by the mine owners.

Within the next two or three decades, the Company put up a considerable amount of cottages in the vicinity of their pits. On the main road leading to Hynds Farm on the Lochore Estate, for example, rows of houses, amounting to almost a hundred individual dwellings, were now occupied by the company's men and their families. Dandy Row and Candle-Makers Row, stood on the site which today holds the village bowling green, and Caravan Row, so called because the roofs of the houses resembled those of a caravan, were all built at this juncture, and it is reasonable to say that the mining village of Lochore dates from this time.

The Capledrae Cannel Coal Company continued to expand, and by 1867 when they were negotiating the lease of part of the Lochore Estate with Lady Scott, their directors now included, amongst others, the advocate James Aytoun, and Crombie and Anderson of Lochgelly, who had money invested in the Balgreddie Colliery.

Lochore Estate was duly sold for £60,000 and the company, by now selling the majority of their coal to the Kinross and Milnathort Gas Company at 14/- per ton, renamed itself the Lochore and Capledrae Coal Company (Ltd).

By 1871, a further two pits and a mine had been sunk. The first, the No. 1 pit, stood a little to the north of where eventually the 'Mary' would be, and reached a depth of some fathoms. The No. 2 pit was situated to the north of the present-day Country Park Centre, and was 47 fathoms deep.

The mine produced mainly ironstone and all in all the company now had a workforce of over a hundred miners and a score of surface workers, and had an approximate daily output of forty tons of 'parrot' coal and fourteen tons of ironstone.

With the coming of the Railways, the age-old method of transporting the coal and ironstone by horse tramway to Kelty gave way to more practical and economic methods, and the ever-expanding Company sunk a further two surface mines before 1879.

One of these stood on the south side of the road which led to Chapel Farm, close to where the 'Mary' No. 2 shaft would stand, in years to come. The second pit sat directly opposite this, on the north of the chapel road, halfway up Bowhouse bank. The remains of the workings can still be seen to this day. A third mine was put down some time after this at Miller's Neuk, to the south of Lochore House.

The mines at Crosshill, which the Company took over in the 1880's along with the Milton pit, had begun operations in 1865 and had a workforce of fifteen, producing eighteen tons daily from the seams of parrot coal. The Milton, which had been sunk in 1869, employed a score of men and extracted coal of such high quality, that it was used for producing gas.

Now managed by Alexander Burns, the company had shipping ports throughout the country, at Burntisland, Leith, Glasgow, Greenock and Alloa, from where their coal and ironstone was exported to every part of the globe.

The Lochore and Capledrae Cannel Coal Company had risen from its somewhat humble beginnings in 1835, to become one of the United Kingdom's largest coal producers in 1890, but later it sold out to the Fife Coal Company who took over the Surface Mine at Benarty.

The smaller Rosewell Gas Coal Company, which had also been producing coal in the area for a number of years, also sold out to the Fife Coal Company, although it did not do so until July 1905, some five years after the purchase of the Lochore and Capledrae Cannel Coal Company.

The Rosewell, at its peak, had operated three shafts and a surface mine close to the NBR Railway lines at Loanhead Avenue and Flockhouse Row. These pits ceased production in 1889.

The Fife Coal Company had been formed in 1872, primarily to work the Kelty collieries, which at that time were producing somewhere in the region of 70,000 tons annually. In the following few years the Company would acquire several other going concerns, the Leven and Pirnie Coalfields, the

Wellsgreen Dysart fields, Hill of Beath and Dalbeath Collieries, as well as the Cowdenbeath and Lumphinnans Pits, seeing their annual output soar to three quarters of a million tons by the turn of the century.

With the Aitken (Kelty) Kirkford and Lumphinnans XI coming into operation. The Fife and Kinross Coal Company were then taken over in 1901 followed by Rosewell, then property at Valleyfield. The Donibristle Colliery Company followed in 1908 and then the Bowhill Coal Company in 1909.

The Fife Coal Company thus consolidated its position as the dominating force in the Fife Coal Industry.

Glencraig Born

During the 19th century, other Mining companies were making inroads in the district, and a considerable amount of time and money was being spent on investigations on the estate of Glencraig to establish whether 'deep' mining would be viable there or not.

The area in the vicinity of Glencraig House had been mined for centuries, and maps from the early Victorian period show scores of abandoned ironstone workings, which were 'ancient' by this time. Several attempts were made by various speculators, in particular George Constable, whose family bought the estate in the middle part of the century, to establish the existence of rich coal seams deep in the ground. Initial tests, however, seemed to indicate that, while there was indeed coal to be had there, the quality was rather poor, as it appeared to be badly burned and virtually useless in the seams located beside the Nellie pit all the way towards Glencraig. This situation was thought to be the same in the Glencraig field itself, and consequently, George Constable received only one firm offer for the land.

Sir John Wilson of Airdrie, acting for the Wilson and Clyde Coal Company bought Glencraig in 1893, and almost immediately ordered the sinking of another two test bores, under the supervision of a Mr W.H. Telfer. These tests proved satisfactory, and, on March 11th, 1895, Mr Telfer cut the ceremonial first sod on the site of what was to be the deepest mine in the country, when coal mining began there in 1897.

On 11th March 1895 the same Mr Telfer cut the first sod at No. 2 Pit (Wee Pit), and about seven weeks later the sinking of No. 1 Pit commenced. After the pits were sunk to the Lochgelly Splint seam, actual coal mining commenced in 1897. In 1899 mines were driven right down to the Dunfermline Splint seam, passing through the seams of the Glassee, Mynheer, and the Five Feet; these were all good navigation coals. Now although Mr Telfer supervised the sinking of both shafts, the Colliery Manager in 1895 was a Mr George McLellan who left the Colliery in April 1898. Mr Telfer was then appointed manager. Still only 26 years old, he served both as manager and agent until November 1910 and resided in Glencraig House, where five of his seven children were born.

For the first three years, steam and household coal was produced from the Lochgelly Splint, Lochgelly Parrot and Jersey seams, but later when the Glassee, Mynher and Five Feet seams were worked they proved to be a very rich navigation coal, and for many years, they provided a large proportion of the colliery output.

Large quantities went to Glasgow to fuel the Atlantic Liners, and Glencraig was also on the Admiralty list for quality navigation coal. Its steam coal was also of a very high quality, and was in great demand by the Railway Companies of the day and used only for their express trains. As for its Splint coal, this was in demand by the whisky distillers during the malting season and 600 tons were despatched weekly to the northern distilleries. Glencraig Colliery would reach coal seams as deep as 240 fathoms and produce a very rich navigation coal within its first few years of existence, and by its peak would employ over 1,500 men and women, with an output of 6,000 tons per week.

Prior to 1895, the only houses at Glencraig were at the quaintly named Contle Row, which had stood since the late 17th century and was known locally as the village of Contihill when they had been part of the Cluniecraig Estate. Events moved swiftly after 1895, and both North and South Glencraig were established, as houses were erected near the Colliery.

A water supply system, whereby water was pumped from a source in the pit and pumped up to a water tank on the pithead gear, from where it was piped directly into every house in the area, was provided by the company, a remarkable achievement for the times, when you consider that most houses elsewhere had to rely on the roadside standpipe or local wells for their water supplies!

And Now The 'Mary'

The period around the turn of the century, in general was one of huge economic and industrial expansion, and Great Britain had become a major

Glencraig Pit No's 1 and 2

Glencraig Pit No's 1 and 2

industrial power, with a huge wealth of natural resources to exploit both at home and throughout the 'Empire'. The 'Workshop of the World' was the United Kingdom, and coal fuelled that 'workshop' as never before. Modern methods of mining were pushing production to untold heights and the Coalfields of Fife were at the forefront of it all.

When the Fife Coal Company took over the workings on the Lochore Estate along with the other pits from the now defunct Lochore and Capledrae Coal Company, it found itself in possession of the surface mine and shaft at Benarty, along with another one at Lochore. Neither of those at Benarty had been worked extensively, whilst operations at the Lochore Pit had been restricted to the Cannel Coal seams, which lay relatively close to the surface.

The new owners wasted little time in drawing up plans for the mining of the deeper seams, rich in Navigation Splint, and the five foot coal seams, which they discovered, extended from their existing Aitken and Lumphinnans pits towards the Ballingry Parish.

Plans were soon in operation to sink a shaft, some 300 fathoms deep, in order to reach these seams, and also to connect them to the workings of the Aitken Pit, thus providing adequate ventilation for the new venture.

By all accounts, March 1st 1902, was a fine and a pleasant Spring day, as a party of the company's directors, their wives, and several local dignitaries set off from Kelty Station, in a specially decorated train, (the engine was hung with green and red flags for the occasion!). From Kelty, the party travelled along the Mineral Line, a distance of just over a mile, to where the new pit was to be sited. Hundreds of local people turned out that spring morning to witness the Managing Director's wife, Mrs Carlow, cut the first turf of the new pit, which would be christened the 'Mary', in her honour.

That week's edition of the 'Dunfermline Journal' relates:-

"Another step has been taken in connection with the development of the minerals of Beath and Ballingry. The first sod of a great new pit which is to be sunk by the Fife Coal Company Limited, in the basin of the Lochore Coalfield was cut on Saturday... by Mrs Carlow, the wife of the managing director of the Company, and the pit is one about halfway between Lochore Castle and Benarty Hill, and near to the solum of the deep loch which was drained fully a century ago. The pit is expected to be 28 feet by 11 feet, and it is expected that it will reach a depth of 300 fathoms before Aitken Navigation Splint coal is struck".

The Mary Pit was to be a show piece for all that was great in modern mining

Mary Pit No. 1

Mary Pit No's 1 and 2

techniques. The pumping engine, built by Douglas and Grant of Kirkcaldy, would be a compound condensing one, with a high pressure cylinder of 58 inches, and a 100 inch low pressure, with a 12 feet stroke. The 'crab' would be capable of raising 50 tons.

The '**Journal**' report continued

"...all the pumping gear will be on the same gigantic scale as the engine and the crab. From a depth of 300 fathoms it is computed that it will raise 1,300 gallons of water per minute".

The great pulleywheels, which would eventually surmount the pithead frame, had been designed specifically for the 'Mary' by the managing director, Charles Carlow, and were to be built by the Krupps Works in Germany, as no British company could be found to produce them to Carlow's specifications.

The estimated cost of the new shaft would be in excess of £100,000, and the work would take approximately four years to complete.

Yet more building work, to provide housing for the incoming workers, was also begun. Additional cottages were erected on the old Hynds Farm site, and the original farmhouse itself was converted into several small flats. Renovation work was carried out on some of the older cottages in Caravan Row, by now renamed Lochleven Road, and on the old farm itself, one of the buildings was converted into a social hall. 'Hynds' hall, as it would be known, soon became the centre for all manner of social gatherings and activities in the early years of the village.

Mary Row, which had been built recently, opposite the new mine, was also expanded (This too would change its name, eventually becoming Peveril Place) and it seemed that Lochore could now look forward to a period of prosperity such as it had never before known.

N.B. The majority of the research into the early coal mines was carried out by Michael Moyles and Jim Mackie of the Heritage Group.

CHAPTER 2

Growing Fast—The Early Years

During W.H. Telfer's tenure as Manager and Agent of Glencraig in the first decade of the new century, the communities surrounding Glencraig Colliery, like many others in the Fife Coalfields, witnessed a period of unprecedented growth. The Wilson and Clyde Coal Company built no less than four hundred houses in and around the village of Glencraig*, whilst private enterprise was largely responsible for the creation of a main street littered with small shops and businesses, the keystone of which was the branch of the Lochgelly Cooperative Society.

In 1904, a school was opened on the southern perimeter of the village, and its classrooms gradually filled with the children of what could be called 'immigrant' workmen, the miners who had been forced to move from the near exhausted seams of the coalfields of Ayrshire, Lanarkshire and Stirlingshire. Along with them came the men from the dying shale mines of the Lothians, and the former agricultural workers from Perth and Angus, all seeking steady work at the new pit. Irish labourers and miners from the north-east of England, all made their way to West Fife, in the early years of the century.

Is it any wonder, then, that with so much newcomers, each determined to preserve their own cultures and traditions, their own way of life, as it were, and all living in close proximity to one another in the miners' rows, that certain frictions came to the force from time to time? Minor squabbles and fights quite often found themselves featured on the pages of the 'Dunfermline Journal', along with the resulting Court appearances of the offenders!

In an article first published in 1908, one of the paper's feature writers leaves his readers in no doubt as to his feelings on the matter.

"...In any case, the fact has got to be faced that many of the inhabitants are of anything but settled habits, and that many more are decidedly ill-behaved. Drinking and gambling are the two principal vices. Wild scenes on the highway are of weekly occurrence, as pay day comes around, and the police have sometimes a hot time. The existing public-house accommodation is inadequate for the needs of the district, and congestion, with its resulting rowdyism, is frequently rampant..."

Footnote: *Glencraig Village lay in two separate parishes, South Glencraig in Auchterderran Parish and North Glencraig in the Parish of Ballingry. Births, deaths and marriages were therefore recorded in different places, Lochgelly in the case of South Glencraig and Crosshill for North Glencraig.

It is perhaps worth pointing out, at this juncture, that a 'Gothenburg' Public House had been opened in North Glencraig in 1901, and two others had followed shortly after this, at Crosshill and Lochore.*

Religion

From the earliest days of the migration of men (and women!) to work the pits at Glencraig, and the Mary at Lochore, some form of worship, relative to their own particular religious persuasion was generally available to most people. The nearby Burgh of Lochgelly, for example, could at that time, amongst other things, boast a Chapel and a Catholic school (St Patrick's), and it would be reasonable to assume that a large percentage of Catholics living in or near Glencraig would worship here. Practicing Catholics from Crosshill and Lochore had to wait until 1908 before they could hear Mass said locally, in Greenwells Cottage, on Ballingry Road, the home of Father Mulherran. Local Catholic children, however, still had to attend the school at Lochgelly, if they were to be brought up in the faith, **Arthur McGachie** recalls.

"As we were Roman Catholics, or R.C., in those far off days, our parents were adament that we must go to the Catholic school, and that meant we had to go to St. Patrick's at Lochgelly. There were no trams or buses then, of course, and we had to walk to and from school each day, a distance of four miles, which I thought was sheer cruelty!"

It was not until 1914, with the opening of St. Kenneth's school, next to Mucklestane Cottage in Crosshill, that the children of Catholic families could be educated locally. St. Kenneth's school was modified so that it could be used as a church on Sundays and Father Mulherran could now say Mass here, instead of at his home, in Mucklestane Cottage, as had happened previously.

Those inhabitants who were of the Protestant persuasion, had since 1893, been able to attend services at the Flockhouse Mission Hall at the top of Lochore, under the ministry of the Reverend Charles Mason, of the Free Church of Portmoak, or there was always the parish church at Ballingry.

In 1904, a new church was erected at Lochcraig, and the Flockhouse portion of the Free Church of Portmoak transferred there. Rev. Mason was a familiar sight in the district, travelling to and fro in a 'Pony and Trap', or by bicycle,

Footnote: * Apart from the 'Goth' in North Glencraig there was also soon to be Hunters Inn at South Glencraig.

to administer to his ever growing flock, as he did every day. It was not until 1909, a year after Charles Mason was officially recognised as the minister of Glencraig and Lochore, that a manse was built for him and his family.

A very different form of transport was made available to Mr Telfer. In 1905, his employers provided him with what was probably the districts first motor car. Not a new one, of course, but nevertheless a mode of transport befitting his role in local society. The motor car they provided for him had no hood and no windscreen, and therefore offered absolutely no protection from the elements. By all accounts, it could only travel uphill very slowly, and in fact, even flat roads had to be negotiated at a snail's pace. One particular incident that Telfer himself recalled some years later, illustrates the vehicles lack of speed: Telfer's driver, John

W. Telfers Car

Duncan, was taking Mr and Mrs Telfer to Lochgelly one afternoon, and the car was 'crawling' up the Station Brae, attracting the attention of some local schoolboys, who began running (or more probably, walking) — alongside it. Much to the extreme embarrassment of John Duncan, the boys began a running commentary on the car's lack of speed. One of the boys, no doubt to the great amusement of his cronies, shouted "Hie Johnny, gie it the whup, mun!"

In **W.H. Telfer's** own words: *"I think after that John Duncan had no great love for that car"*. However, despite incidents like this, Mr Telfer later said of his time at Glencraig, *"Our twelve and a half years residence here was a happy time for us, as we both liked Fife, and Glencraig, and we retained pleasant memories of this district and of the many good friends we had.*

Personally, I enjoyed those years of close association with the Management of Glencraig Colliery, and the friendly relationship with the officials and workmen, most of whom I knew personally in those days".

Typhoid Epidemic

The miners cottages which had been built at Glencraig, as stated earlier, had their own water supply piped directly to them, from a water tank at the new Colliery, but no such 'luxury' was afforded to the inhabitants of Lochore, and it was here, in the summer months of 1903, that an epidemic of typhoid fever broke out.

The **'Dunfermline Journal'** contained several reports on the outbreak:- (This from the issue dated July 11th):

"Two more deaths occurred on Thursday from typhoid fever at Lochore. During the week, altogether four new cases were notified. The district, in circumference of three or four miles, has a curious odour arising from the disinfectants. A considerable number of people have left the district since the epidemic broke out, and many houses are vacant".

It seems that this particular outbreak began at about the same time as the Fife Coal Company installed a new water-tank at the Mary for the miners to fill their flasks from. The people living in Mary Row also had access to this water supply for their daily needs. Unfortunately, the water in the tank came from the nearby Ladath Burn, which passed by an open ash pit, near to the steading at Lochore House. Consequently, the water became contaminated by the ash pit, and by the end of July, twenty one cases of typhoid had been reported to the authorities.

A fresh source of water was obtained from a spring some distance away from the Ladath Burn, but this too became infected, and within a matter of a few weeks at least fifteen local people had lost their lives, and a further one hundred and fifty people had been admitted to Thornton Hospital. In the House of Commons, the M.P. for West Fife, **John Hope,** raised the issue with the Secretary of State for the Home Department, and asked him:

"...if his attention had been called to the outbreak of typhoid fever near Lochgelly, Fifeshire, in houses recently built by the Fife Coal Company for their workmen, and if he would institute an enquiry into all the circumstances in view of the loss of life which had taken place..."

The **Minister of State** replied,

"...I am informed... by His Majesty's Inspector of Mines for the East of Scotland district, that active measures have been taken to prevent any further spread of the epidemic. Pure water is being taken in carts to the locality; persons attacked are at once removed to the hospital; and disinfection is being carried out. The local authority is also stated to be considering the question of a new

scheme of water supply. Only one fresh case has been notified since Saturday, so it is hoped that the measures taken have been successful in checking the outbreak".

Steps were indeed being taken to alleviate the suffering. The Fife Coal Company paid for the services of two nurses to care for the victims of the epidemic, and a relief fund was initiated to help those families who had suffered the most. The company advanced money to this Fund and proposals were made regarding the introduction of a safe, permanent water supply to the village. Eventually a water supply was piped into Lochore from Lochgelly, at a cost of 8d (approximately 3½ new pence) per thousand gallons, and this was the method that was used until after the First World War, when a supply was brought to the village from Glenfarg. Epidemics such as the 1903 one would now, thankfully, be confined to the dark days of history, as far as Lochore was concerned.

Between 1901, when, according to the National Census of that year, the combined population of the villages of Glencraig, Crosshill and Lochore stood at 1,500, and 1908, when it was estimated that upwards of 6,500 people had made the district their home, further important developments took place. 1910 saw the opening of a Miners' Institute in Lochore and in the following year the Institute added a hall to its premises, so that public meetings and social gatherings could take place there.

Pit Developments

Glencraig Colliery, by 1911, was employing almost 1,300 men — 1,043 working underground, and a further 224 on the surface. Telfer's reign as manager had given way in 1909 to that of Robert Wilson. Coal production was now in excess of 6,000 tons weekly.

The men working the seams operated the 'pick place' method, whereby one of a team of two miners stripped the coal from the face with his pick, whilst the other man would fill the hutch, push it out to a central point, and return with an empty hutch. Many of these 'pick places' were worked by father and son teams, each pair being paid according to the tonnage produced. Each pick place had its own recognised 'pin' or 'tab', usually a piece of string with a stamped disc, or washer etc. that marked the site and identified it as belonging to one particular team. These tabs were removed when the hutch was weighed at the pithead, and the coal credited accordingly. This method continued until the early 1920s when the 'Pan Runs' began.

As the Mary Pit developed, its output increased gradually, until it eventually equalled that of the Lindsay Pit at Kelty — some 250,000 tons a year. By 1911, the Mary employed 747 below ground and 154 on the surface.

Community Growth

Above ground, the village community was growing and gradually those 'immigrant' families of a few years previously began to knit together to form a strong and close community. The places of worship, which now included the Bethany Hall, were a source of comfort to many, whilst the formation of a Junior Football club, Glencraig Celtic, gave many more a common allegiance.

Glencraig Celtic F.C.

The club had been formed in 1905 to play in the Fifeshire Junior League and within the first few years of its existence, the 'Celtic' had made their presence known, winning no less than fifteen trophies by 1915. The Fifeshire Junior Cup, the Cowdenbeath Cup, the West Fife Cup and the Fife Shield all fell to the village. Over the years Glencraig Celtic supplied many players to Senior clubs, not only in Scotland, but all over Britain.

Prominent amongst those was Peter Johnstone, who joined Glasgow Celtic and was 'capped' against the Irish League in 1915. Unfortunately, Peter lost his life in the First World War.

Whilst the menfolk had their football, or other 'sporting pursuits', the women of the village knew no form of social life except for their visits to the Co-op, or 'The Store' as it was known. The 'Store' was at the very heart of village life. A place where the women, apart from doing their shopping, could meet to hear the latest village 'news' being told, and quite often retold with much embellishment.

The demands for adequate shopping facilities in the area had increased with the numbers of workers and their families who came to work in the new pits. The demand was met to a large extent by the Lochgelly Co-operative Society, already well established in Lochgelly itself, who opened several departments in South Glencraig. The Co-op's bakery, butchers, drapers and hardware departments were housed in purpose built premises built just south of the Ore Bridge.

The Lochgelly Co-op quickly followed this by setting up further shops at both Lochore and Crosshill. The Lochore 'Store' comprised of a grocery department, a bakery, butchery and hardware store, while the 'Store' at Crosshill brought amongst other things, a chemists dispensary.

Kelty Co-operative Society set up a shop in Crosshill in 1906, at the present day entrance to the 'Meadows'. This two-storey building featured a dual-purpose shop on the ground floor, housing a grocery department alongside that of their hardware branch. Other departments were opened shortly after the end of the First World War in Hope Terrace, Lochore. The extending of the Tramways, from Landale Street in Lochgelly to the D.C.I. Buildings in Lochore, in December 1912, brought with it the opportunity, to both young and old, to travel more regularly.

The trams meant easy access to Lochgelly Station and therefore, easier access to Dunfermline, Edinburgh and beyond. To the young women of Glencraig, Crosshill and Lochore, the factories of Dunfermline, now reasonably easy to get to thanks to the trams, became a more desirable alternative to working on the Pit-head or going into 'service'. To the miner's wife, the tramway offered the opportunity to shop in the larger towns, such as Cowdenbeath, and no longer would she be prepared to settle for the village store to provide all weekly shopping requirements. Cowdenbeath was fast becoming a thriving and attractive shopping centre and people from all the surrounding villages made their way there on Saturday afternoons.

The outlying districts of Lochore, Glencraig and Crosshill depended not only on the tram car for these 'special' shopping expeditions, but also, like any other community founded on coal-mining, on the steady turn of the companies' pulley wheels. Strikes and lock-outs made the shopping trips to Cowdenbeath and beyond however a very remote possibility. Only a full week's work for her 'man' would allow the miner's wife this luxury. During the very many spells of 'broken time', many women were content simply to spend a couple of hours walking up and down Cowdenbeath High Street, 'window shopping', having managed only to save the few coppers required for the return ticket. Soon, most would have to postpone even this trip, as 1912 came in and the miners faced the prospect of a National Strike.

· CHAPTER 3 ·

From Slaves to Soldiers

Before looking specifically at the 1912 Miners Strike it is important to trace back the historical position of Miners and their families and how they were treated by those in power.

For centuries, the miner and his family had faced a continuing battle against appalling living conditions and desperately poor wages. For many hundreds of years, the nation's coal supply had been gained at a cost of great hardship and suffering to the miner. It is worthwhile here looking at their background.

Until 1775 colliers were serfs in the fullest sense of the word. Writes the historian of the Alloa Coal Co:

"They were cut off by the brand of slavery from their fellow men. They were bound by the mine in which they worked, and were sold as part of the working machinery. . . the child of the collier was almost certainly a slave from his earliest years, starting work at the age of eight or nine and remaining in the pit for periods of sixteen to eighteen hours. The wives and daughters of the colliers were employed as human beasts of burden to carry up the coal from the pit. Legal serfdom was ended in 1779, not so much from a desire to remove the reproach of slavery in a free country, as from the anxiety to attract a larger number of workers to the rapidly-expanding coal industry".

In the early 17th century, the need for coal was so great and manpower in the pits so scarce that an Act of Parliament, condemning the miner to slavery, had been passed. This Act remained on the Statutes for almost 200 years, before being repealed in 1799.

As the 19th century dawned, the British Government, greatly concerned by the bloody revolution across the English Channel, took steps to ensure that a similar situation would not arise here. A series of 'Combination' Acts were passed forbidding workers from combining together to better their conditions. At a time when massive expansions were taking place in the coal industry to meet the demands of the Industrial revolution, these new laws ensured that the vast profits being made by the wealthy coal owners would not be affected by industrial action on the part of the miners.

Discontent at the harsh conditions and low wages was echoed in the increase in the numbers of 'underground' societies. The Chartist movement and very early trade unions began to appear, despite the repressive measures being taken to smash the power of the workers. One of the earliest miners' unions, the Colliers' Union, which was formed in 1817, managed to make a mockery of the Combination Laws by holding their meetings in public, and changing their officials at every meeting.

Once the hated Combination Laws had finally been repealed in 1824, a number of small unions began to appear in the coal industry. Though usually of a highly temporary nature, and generally exclusive to one pit or another, these newly formed unions were to be the forerunners of the larger nationwide federations and eventually the N.U.M. Gradually, the smaller 'one-pit' unions began to merge with one another to become 'county' unions, concerned not with merely local issues, but with all the miners' working conditions throughout the area.

By 1870, the miners of Clackmannan had thrown in their lot with those in Fife to form the Fife and Clackmannan Miners Association, and, in that year of the Franco-Prussion War, inaugurated the first ever eight hour working day. Previously, shifts of ten or eleven hours, earning the miner a miserable 3/- a day, had been the norm. The F.C.M.A. attached a condition of membership, by which no member would work more than eight hours at a stretch. Considering the small wages, coupled with the fact that long hours continued to be worked in the great coal-producing fields of Lanarkshire, Ayrshire and the Lothians, the step taken by the miners of Fife and Clackmannan was a brave and bold one. From the first Monday in June, 1870, the eight hour shift became a reality in the mines of Fife and Clackmannan.

Just as the small, local unions came together to form county unions, so, eventually, did those county ones join with others, building into a Federation of Scottish Mineworkers, largely due to the influence of one Alexander McDonald, himself a former mineworker, who rose to be the M.P. for Stafford in the 1870s. This was 'The Spring-Tide Of Trade Unionism' — a period which saw the miners gain some notable victories in their fight for better conditions. There were setbacks as well, however. The great economic crisis of 1879 brought wage cuts, strikes, lock outs and evictions amongst the mining communities.

Victimisation was rife, as union after union was systematically destroyed, or driven underground, until, by 1880, only the Fife and Kinross Miners' Association survived.

The revival of the union movement came largely due to the efforts of James

Keir Hardie. In 1886, Keir Hardie became Secretary of the newly formed Scottish Miners' National Federation, and saw at once the weaknesses of a loose federation of various unions. By 1889, after successive conferences and consultations with miners' leaders, the Miner's Federation of Great Britain was born. Now, at long last, the men who drew the coal, had a national voice. No longer would the coal owners be quite so able to 'divide and defeat', as they had done so often in the past. It had taken a century of struggle to free themselves, finally, from the bondage imposed on them and their families, and this freedom would not be yielded lightly.

One final word on the early struggle for recognition of the miners rights should be made here. For centuries, the men of the mines, and their families, were looked on as being little more than vagabonds, not only by their employers, but also by their fellow villagers. In one county of Scotland, even in death the miner was not allowed the same rights as even the poorest of his neighbours were. The miners in that county were not allowed to be buried in the same churchyard as other 'more respectable' folk, a situation which carried on until well into the 19th century. That county incidentally, was Fife!

First National Strike

The Miner's strike of 1912 lasted just over six weeks, and was significant in that it was the first National Miners Strike that Great Britain had ever known. Every single pit in the country came out on strike, and it was this, probably, more than any other development that forced the Government of the day to introduce legislation to bring about a National Minimum Wage structure for the mining industry.

With this assurance, and the promise of the coal owners to take part in district wage negotiations, the men eventually returned to work in April 1912. It was to prove only a partial victory.

The gains made by the miners in the aftermath of the 1912 strike were very limited. Nevertheless, the strike had proved once and for all that the men who manned the coal mines could, when the need arose, organise themselves into a force that could successfully fight for better conditions and a fairer way of life. This had not always been the case, and can be seen from the earlier part of this chapter.

However, in the weeks and months following the strike, coal production rose steadily, as it became obvious to most people that the country was stock-piling assets in preparation for the war in Europe that now seemed inevitable.

Miners' leaders, along with the Labour Party, saw it as their duty to do all in their power to prevent war breaking out. They, along with others saw the coming struggle not as a military engagement against a foreign power, but as a class struggle, in which the working men and women all over Europe should stand together and fight for their own needs, rather than be used, as pawns in International conflicts.

As late as August 1914, when all seemed lost, the Socialist leader, **Keir Hardie** issued one last cry from the heart *"Workers, stand together... for peace. Combine and conquer the militarist enemy and self-seeking Imperialists today, once and for all.*

Men and women of Great Britain you now have an unexampled opportunity of rendering a magnificent service to humanity, and to the world.

Proclaim that for you the days of plunder and butchery have gone by. Send messages of peace and fraternity to your fellows who have less liberty than you. Down with class rule. Down with the rule of brute force. Down with war. Up with the peaceful rule of the people".

The call, like so many others, was in vain. Events in far off Sarajevo had overtaken the peace-movement, and a torrent of war fever, unsurpassed by anything in the past swept the country, as thousands of workers rushed to enlist. For millions of men and women life would never be the same again.

The First World War

When war broke out in the summer months of 1914 young men from all parts of the country were quick to 'answer the call', and those who lived in the villages of Lochore, Glencraig and Crosshill were no exception. Glencraig had, like so many other villages throughout the British Isles, its own recruiting 'agent' — one John McGovern, a retired sergeant from the Black Watch, who at the time was employed as a janitor at one of the local schools. No doubt a great many of Glencraig's volunteers took 'the King's shilling' from Mr McGovern.

Alex 'Whup' Robertson, later in life, a stalwart Secretary of Lochore Welfare Junior F.C., was one of those young men who 'answered the call of duty' and enlisted in the forces. Mr Robertson, who had worked as the Mary Pit Officer, from the age of fourteen, still has in his possession a railway ticket issued to him during the war, when he was travelling home on leave. The ticket allowed Mr Robertson to travel from Paris to Lochgelly Station! Alex Robertson was a boy of seventeen when he volunteered for the army.

By November, the '**Dunfermline Journal**' estimated that at least 500 men from the district had volunteered for armed service.

"*...from Glencraig over 200 men have joined the colours, the number being a little less than that of the Lochore and Crosshill Miners.*

A curious fact which one discovers over practically the whole of West Fife district is that the greater portion of the whole men enlisted are married men who have left behind them families of fairly large dimensions. It naturally follows that there must be a considerable amount of distress and the agencies at work trying to alleviate the poverty and misery due to the war, have a very busy time. The principal burden in this respect has fallen upon the Soldiers and Sailors' Association, who have filled the gap until the receipt by dependants of seperation allowances. This Association has, to date, relieved over two hundred cases of distress and many instances could be cited where the misery has been very acute indeed.

The collieries in the district have so far continued to give regular employment. Glencraig Pit has only lost four shifts since the outbreak of hostilities, although it may be mentioned that owing to the cessation of trade with Germany, the anthracite section of the Colliery has to be suspended. In Lochore, the Mary Pit is now working single shift instead of double shift, but the work is plentiful, and many miners from Lochgelly and other districts have flocked in to take the places of those who have gone to the front.

... The regularity of employment is having the effect of keeping many from joining the colours, who otherwise would from force of circumstances have been more inclined to do so".

The article continues...

"*The effect is most strongly felt when the officials come to deal with cases of distress. The miners have long been accustomed to large pays in times of prosperity*"

It is at this point that the article, far from being merely a general description of village life during war-time, turns to its real nature — an out and out attack on the Mining classes. It continues...

"*They have lived in a state of comparative affluence. They allowed themselves to want for nothing that money could procure for them, and earning a wage that many a professional man cannot command they have unfortunately lived to the full extent of their income and for them the wisdom of saving for a rainy day did not exist. Even in times of prosperity, a slack week or fortnight found them pulling their waist-belt a little tighter. Thus it comes about that many wives — old and young — are most improvident and cannot spend a pound to the full advantage; the habit of thrift is totally unknown to them, and in the present circumstances when money is scarce and food dear they cannot break away from former habits and inclinations. This may appear to be sweeping indictment, but it is unfortunately only too clearly proved by the investigations made in regard to cases of distress. Examples innumerable could be cited. One woman with three of a family had a weekly income from the Government of 24s. and still she found reason to complain that she could not make ends meet. Another woman was given a ticket enabling her to get goods to the value of 5s. from a grocer, and with that ticket she produced only four articles and those articles the best of everything.*

Shortly after the outbreak nearly fifty percent of the total number who have enlisted left the district and immediately the wives began to make calls upon the pawnbroker, and article by article the furniture of the homes began to disappear. The officials in charge of the schemes for alleviating distress, when they learned of such cases, called upon the parties and endeavoured by small supplies of money to make up the leeway. In other cases they attempted by a little homely counsel to make the women understand that plainer and cheaper food would be the best policy until more money was available, but to little purpose. The wives of the absent men took up the attitude that the advice was not required or would not be listened to. One woman who was complaining about hard times could only stare when informed that many a good strong health-giving plate of soup could be made from marrow bones. The women themselves do nothing to help, but simply sit at home and wait on the arrival of the separation allowance.

Of course it musn't be imagined for a moment that these allegations are directed against the whole of the miner's wives in the district. There are quite a number of frugal thrifty women who are willing to scrape and save in order to make ends meet at this critical time, but unfortunately that type of wife is in a decided minority.''

The highly moral nature of the article is common to most newspapers of the time. The country was at war, and most editors and feature writers saw it as their duty to be above all, patriotic, and supportive of all the 'authorities' did and said. Those who joined the Colours were heroes; any man who did not enlist was looked on as being at best a coward, at worst a traitor to his country. It takes little imagination to see how the readers of this article would believe it unreservedly. Most families had at least one member in the armed forces, and did not take kindly to the thought that other people were profiting from others bravery. As a piece of 'black propaganda' this article would no doubt have succeeded in once more turning public against the miner.

It goes on . . .

It is a curious fact that the most of such cases came from Lochore, and in that village also the charitable organisations found the widest field for their labours. Indeed there is a vast difference between the communities of Glencraig and Lochore. In the former, the inhabitants are of a settle, steady disposition, men who have lived in the district for many years, and worked in the same colliery all their life. In Lochore, on the other hand, the bulk of the population is composed of a most migratory class of miner — here today and away tomorrow. There is even a striking difference in the style of houses which compose the two villages. Those of Glencraig are more substantially built, much more cleanly in their appearance than the dirty brick built rows which form the biggest part of Lochore. There is in existence, also in the community, as doubtless in many others, a system of co-operation in the buying of goods. One woman will obtain a credit book for use at a co-operative institution and through the book will supply neighbours with goods, herself as being the owner of the book guaranteeing payment of all the goods she receives. Thus it happens that when money is scarce she cannot clear her book and is refused goods, this step affecting probably three or four families who, not being in possession of sufficient ready cash cannot obtain goods elsewhere, thus causing starvation and distress. This practice is carried out unknown to the officials of the Co-operative Institution. Those responsible for the distribution of S. and S.F.A. (Soldiers & Sailors Families Association) allowances have also been troubled by many claims which on enquiry were proved not to be genuine.

The writer then goes on to deal with the differences between the 'decent' native-born families and their 'immigrant' counterparts (i.e. the Irish, English and in some cases Polish workers who had come to the district looking for steady work)

Owing to the large number of married men who have left the district, work is being delegated to unmarried and comparatively young men who are thus finding themselves with considerably increased incomes. Quite a number of the young miners in Fife, instead of being like sons in a house, are rather in the light of lodgers, paying a fixed sum to their parents in lieu of board and lodgings. This allowance may have been, in several cases, increased, but the young men still retain quite a considerable sum to be disposed of as they please. There exists in most mining communities an element of gambling — pitch and toss, whippet racing, and such like — and in these forms of sport, a large number of young men find ample outlets for wasting their wages. The police authorities say that while there are many men away drinking and petty crimes go on as usual. It is only forbearance in taking proceedings against some sole remaining bread winners that prevent the Court returns from being much the same as usual.

It will thus be seen, that considering the whole circumstances, the large pays of the miners have in the existing state of affairs become a disadvantage rather than a benefit, and only such circumstances as those arising out of the present war will have the effect of teaching the wasteral women and men frugality and thrift. It is probably a hard, oppressive method, but nevertheless, needful.

The shopkeepers in this district complain along the same lines as those in all other communities, Glencraig is the principle shopping centre and here the grocers, bakers and butchers have reason to deplore a decrease in turnover of almost 25 per cent, while at the same time there is a great increase in the price of material — particularly baking material while at the same time the retailers cannot increase the rates to the consumers. The people are in other ways doing something to help the men at the front, and a fair large quantity of garments have been despatched.

The coal trade is naturally the key to the whole situation. Should work cease there must immediately follow a period of accute distress when the separation allowance given by the Government will not be sufficient to keep the wolf from the door. At present the work is plentiful, but the colliery authorities cannot prophesy as to the future. They are, however, doing what they can, and are allowing dependants of men at the front free rent and coal. The men on the other hand, refused, as in other parts of the country, to agree to a levy on their wages to the National relief fund. On the whole the community is likely to suffer acutely as time goes on".

This article appeared in the 'Journal' on the 21st November, 1914 and the 'jingoism' of the writer can cleary be seen. It was a disgraceful attack on the people in the Mining Communities — their families struggling to survive in desperate circumstances.

The exodus from all corners of industry soon created scarcities of essential materials, not least in the coal trade. By 1917 the situation had become desperate and Lloyd George declared that for the duration of the war, the State would take control of the Mines. This was not nationalisation, but simply Government of output and distribution. State control would have some considerable advantages for the miners. For one thing, it destroyed the claims of the Mine owners that wage disputes could not be settled on a national level, only on a district one. State control struck at the very heart of the owners' constant refusal to negotiate nationally, and at the same time it was to give greater impetus to the miners' calls for nationalisation of the industry. Government control of the pits would last, eventually, until early 1921, its demise heralding one of the most bitter struggles between the miners and their employers.

The number of miners who enlisted created shortages in the mines which had to be filled in many cases by young boys, in their early teens, and women who for the most part, took over a lot of the surface work. **Arthur McGachie**, a boy of 13 in 1917, recalls —

"I attended St. Kenneth's School, and my father died in the war. My mother received the army war pension of 10/- weekly plus an additional 2/- for each child in the family, which meant that in our case my mother had the grand total of £1.2/-d. per week to provide food, clothing, rent and heating for herself and her six children, aged from one year to thirteen years. Many miners joined the forces, and this caused a desperate situation at all the pits. Many women already worked at the pit, so in order to boost their family income, my mother aged 42, started work at the pithead.

By 1917, when I became 13, I applied to the Education Board for exemption from school, so that I too could get work at the pit. My family was having many hungry days, some days we had no food at all and had to visit our Granny down at the Milton Rows, for a meal, or whatever she could give us. My application to the Education Board was granted, the letter arriving at my house on the Thursday, and so I started working the very next day, at 6.00 a.m. For a year I worked at the Pithead, and then I went down the Pit itself".

Arthur's story is, unfortunately, all too common, not only in the Benarty district, but throughout the whole of the country.

The End — At Last

The war, despite the initial prophesy that "it would be all over in six weeks" dragged on for four long years in which millions of men were lost on both sides, virtually a generation wiped out. Eventually having fought to a standstill and weary of the futility of it all, an Armistice was signed on 11 November 1918. The 'War to end Wars' was over and the combatants trudged home, to the promise of a 'Land fit for Heroes'.

But those who returned to the villages of Benarty left behind their share of fallen in the battlefields of France and Flanders. To commemorate their memory, some six years after the Great War, on Saturday 22 March, 1924, to be exact, veterans of the conflict marched from Crosshill village to the Lochore Institute, a lone piper at their head, to pay tribute to the seventy six men from the Mary Pit alone, who had given their lives in the war.

That morning a crowd had gathered to witness the unveiling of a white marble Memorial stone at the Institute to honour the fallen. There were the usual local, and national, dignitaries in the assembly, but the day belonged to the men themselves and the families who had lost husbands, some fathers, in the fight to 'produce a land fit for heroes'.

James Brown, M.P. the Lord High Commissioner to the General Assembly, (the first commoner for centuries to hold that office) told the gathering that he was sure there were many like himself in the crowd who were struggling with emotions they could scarcely keep in check — he himself had lost a son during the war itself, to understand the true value of the sacrifice made by the men *'on the altar of their country'*. The sorrow and sadness, **Mr Brown** continued, could be contained by the memory of their faithfulness, courage and steadfastness even in the face of death.

"These thoughts would encourage us to go forward hopefully to the light of better and brighter times that lie ahead. That we had hopes of better times was due to the valour of that great army which flocked to the Colours to maintain and defend the honour of our plighted word. Memorials such as this were a common bond throughout the great Commonwealth, every name on them inspires us to go forward and live worthily.

To live carelessly and heedlessly, when the world was crying out for strong men and women to save it from despair would surely be a betrayal of trust. To refuse to take our part in the reconstruction of our country and of the world, to bear malice or suspicion or hatred would be a complete betrayal of everything for which our gallant boys laid down their lives".

After the applause died down, a local woman, Nurse Larnoch, stepped forward and unveiled the Memorial. Dr Sinclair, himself an ex-soldier of the '14' war, laid the first wreath, as one by one, the ex-soldiers filed past and saluted the stone. Once the 'Last Post' had been sounded, the Memorial was dedicated by the parish minister, the Reverend G. Scanlon, in what must surely have been one of the most moving ceremonies ever to take place at the Institute.

The white marble stone was engraved with the names of the men from the Mary Colliery who died in the War.

James Bell	Peter Kerr	Neil McCluckie
John Edward Bell	John King	Henry McFarlane
Joseph Bell	Alex. Langlands	William Napier
James Blades	Thomas Logan	James Nellies
James Bogie	John Lynch	George Nixon
John Borland	Archibald Malcolm	John Oatley
Thomas Brown	Charles Martin	William Reilly
George Bruce	James Maxwell	Alex. Rushford
Thomas Casey	James Milne	William Russell
David Close	Daniel Mitchell	Robert Rutherford
John Crawford	Nichol Mitchison	Peter Sharp
Steven Cunningham	Joseph Murphy	James Smith
Peter Devine	Charles McCallum	John Smith
James Duncan	William McCullum	William Smith
Frederick Easterbrook	James McCue	Charles Stewart
William Fotheringham	Alex. McCusker	Sinclair Stewart
Samuel Francis	James McEwen	Thomas Sykes
Charles Fraser	Thomas McFarlane	William Templeman
John Gentles	William McFarlane	Thomas Thomson
John Grinnan	John McGaghie	George Thomson
Alex. Hislop	Thomas McGowan	Robert Walls
Hugh Kane	Hugh McGuire	John West
James Kelly	Peter McKenna	William Wilson
Peter Kelly	Bernard McLinden	John Woods
James Kelly	John McLinden	George Woods
		Henry Young

It is unfortunate that no similar memorial was erected on behalf of the men from Glencraig Colliery who also made the supreme sacrifice in the years of 1914-1918.

CHAPTER 4

A Land Fit For Heroes

The Great War, which would, they said, create a land *'fit for a heroes'*, would, in reality, do no such thing. By 1920, unemployment in the coal-mining and other industries, had reached record levels. For the next twenty years or so the number of men out of work never dropped below the one million mark, and frequently the numbers almost doubled.

For those who had work, life was little better. The four years of war had seen the cost of living rise steadily until it stood at a staggering 142% above the pre-war figure. When the miners asked for a wage increase in early 1920, the Government responded by first offering the men an increase far short of what they had asked for, and secondly by announcing a huge increase in the price of coal, or more especially, the price of household coal. It soon became clear that the Government was deliberately manipulating prices in order to work public opinion towards decontrol of the coal industry, in other words they were preparing to hand back control of the mines to the private sector. The Miners' Unions put forward a second pay claim which they linked with a cut in domestic coal prices. When, once more, the Government flatly rejected this in August 1920, a strike ballot was called and the vast majority of miners (some 73%) voted in favour of strike action.

The strike, when it came, was almost 100%. The 'Datum Line' Strike, as it became known, lasted a little over two weeks and the men returned to work only when an agreement was reached linking wages with output. Advances in wages were to be paid, provided that total production rose above a certain agreed tonnage, known as the Datum Line: this agreement was not to last beyond the winter months of 1920-21.

During the '14-18 war, in an attempt to increase coal production, for the war effort, Lord Sankey, a member of the Tory Government, introduced a special monetary bonus to be paid to all miners on completion of a full week's work. This bonus became known as 'Sankey Money'. Following the 'Datum Line' dispute of 1920, the Government, by 1921, had decided to stop this payment, and asked the miners to sign an agreement, accepting a cut in their living standards. A face worker, for instance, with a wage of £5.0.10d, would, by this agreement, see his weekly pay drop to £3.17.11d — a cut of £1.12.11d.

Naturally, the miners refused to sign any such agreement, and, within a matter of days, found themselves involved in 'lock-outs' all over the country. In the 'Dunfermline Press' of April 1921 the 'ugly situation' which had developed in the Fife Coalfields was reported on at length. The armed forces and the police were drafted in and confrontations took place in Lochgelly, Kelty and Cowdenbeath. In this area, the stoppage was complete. At a mass meeting of the Glencraig and Lochore Miners, the following resolution was passed.

"That this joint meeting of Glencraig and Lochore locked-out miners demand that our National Executive cease negotiations with the coalowners and that the Government give effect to the findings of the Sankey Commission".

In his book, 'My Life With The Miners', **Abe Moffat** describes attempts by the management to disrupt such meetings,

"At Glencraig Colliery the management would blow the horn to prevent the miners hearing us speak. This went on until one day the checkweigher, a very good old militant named Paddy Crossan, decided to stop this practice of the management.

That day when the pit horn blew, Paddy walked off the pithead, went into a private telephone box, and 'phoned the Fire Brigade, as the horn was blowing before its proper time. Down came the Fire Brigade to find Jimmy Stewart and me addressing a pit meeting. Poor Paddy got fined £30 in court for that incident, but it certainly stopped the practice of blowing the pit horn when we were holding meetings".

At first, the Government sent in the Black Watch to the district, but these troops were soon replaced by others with no connection to Fife, namely the Marines, a tough force with little love for the miners.

In nearby Cowdenbeath, for example, the Riot Act was read, and the town itself came under martial law. Cowdenbeath saw many street battles and brutal clashes between the striking miners and the armed forces and police, as the authorities did all in their power to break the strike. The workers leaders were singled out for 'special' attention, by the powers that were and sent to prison.

Eventually, after weeks of lockouts, marches and street battles, the miners were forced by a combination of intimidation, victimisation and pure hunger, to sign the bitterly hated agreement, and take a cut in wages. Later the activists found themselves blacklisted from all the collieries in the bitter aftermath of the strike. In an era when unemployment was to reach record levels, these unfortunate men (and in some cases women) had no chance of finding work in their home areas after being dismissed by the Coal Companies.

The 1921 Strike had also taken its toll of the pits themselves, and many collieries experienced difficulties in returning to normal production due to flood damage, coupled to the need to repair roadways before production could commence.

The Mary Pit was no exception, and by October of 1921 only the upper workings of the Mynheer seam had been re-opened there. In addition the deep workings of the No. 1 shaft at the Mary Colliery had long had a reputation for being uncomfortably warm and the men working the seams very often toiled wearing no more than a pair of short pants.

Prior to the 1921 strike it had been decided to sink the No. 2 shaft, but this had been abandoned when the Strike broke out. With the strike over, the shaft was sunk in 1923, and the ventilation improved throughout the Pit.

The No. 2 shaft was 280 fathoms deep and its pithead frame, one of the first in the country to be constructed of reinforced concrete, stands to this day as a feature of Lochore Meadows Country Park, a permanent reminder of one aspect of Lochore's mining heritage.

After The Strike

With the strike over, things began slowly to return to normal, and amongst other activities it is worth noting that Ambulance classes were organised at the pits; these were certainly very necessary. The mining industry was notorious for accidents. Indeed in 1913, for example, there were 1,580 deaths underground in Scotland as well as 1,273 on the surface. A study of the local press in the first quarter of the century shows that hardly a month went past without a report of some harrowing accident or death at a pit.

However money had to be raised for the equipment and the training of willing volunteers by holding social evenings and other such events. One such social was held in the Goth at Glencraig in March 1925 where Robert Crawford, the agent for the Pit stressed the need for such a service within the industry.

"As mining is an occupation we can never hope to eliminate the element of danger or accident, it is of the utmost importance that in every mine there should be, amongst the workmen themselves, men trained in first-aid who could be capable of affording skilled assistance at the critical moment".

The local physician, Dr Sinclair presented prizes to those men who had successfully completed the first-aid course. Dr Sinclair said that the men could give invaluable aid to anyone unlucky enough to be injured in the pit, helping the doctors etc.

Mary Pit No. 2

With the opening of the Mary No. 2 Pit, the demand for housing increased and in the spring months of 1924, new Fife Coal Company houses were built to accommodate the colliery workers. In addition to these, new houses were erected at Garry Park, Glencraig.

However, the community lost one of its most popular figures in early 1925, when the Reverend Charles Mason passed away. The Reverend Mason who, along with the other religious dignatory in the area, Father Mulheran, were held in awe by most people, churchgoers or not.

Upon his death in January 1925, no less a figure than the **Moderator of the General Assembly of the Church of Scotland** was moved to write a glowing tribute from which the following extracts are taken to indicate his commitment to the community.

"By the death of the Rev. Charles Mason, the Presbytery has lost a member whose whole ministerial life was spent within its bounds, first at Portmoak and then at Glencraig and Lochore. He was ordained in 1893 and died in his

75th year, an old man doing a young man's work in one of the hardest spheres of service in all Scotland.

He came to live in Glencraig, peculiarly fitted for work in a mining community. He was a man of robust health and tireless energy. He had an optimistic temperament. He had a big heart, a clear head, and broad, generous sympathies.

The fragrance of his memory will linger in Glencraig and Lochore, as it lingers still in Kinnesswood and Scotlandwell".

1 9 2 6 G e n e r a l S t r i k e

But the people of Glencraig and Lochore had little time to dwell on such memories, because within a year they were plunged into the greatest industrial strike in the history of Great Britain — The General Strike of 1926. On the first day of May, 1926, after several months of minor (and in some cases not so minor) industrial disputes, the Trade Union Congress of Great Britain called for a General Strike, when, following the Samuel report on the coalmining industry, the coal owners attempted to cut wages and introduce longer working hours.

In the post-war slump of the mid 1920s, Stanley Baldwin's Government had tried to solve the country's financial difficulties at the expense of the working people. Baldwin's cry that **"Wages must come down"**, was taken up by industrialists and businessmen alike, and the Miners were the first to be attacked. Refusal to comply with the Mine owners demands would mean 'lock outs' and sackings at pits throughout the country, and so the Miners' Union leaders had little choice but to call for support from the T.U.C. Response to the General Strike call came from all over the country, as other Union leaders saw what was happening to the miners would almost certainly happen to other trades if the miners' cause was lost.

Railwaymen, transport workers, engineers and men from the ship building industries all rallied to the call, and it seemed that the vast majority of public opinion was behind the strike. The Government reacted swiftly. Prime Minister Baldwin mobilised the armed forces to distribute food and recruited volunteers, as well as the police, to keep essential services running. The police baton-charged picket lines on several occasions up and down the country, and many strike leaders were arrested, and ultimately convicted, on a series of trumped-up charges.

In the face of all these measures, the T.U.C. called off the strike after only nine days, but the miners refused to end their fight, and remained on strike for a further seven months, valiantly struggling for their rallying slogan.

"Not a penny off the pay, not a minute on the day".

Throughout the Fife coalfield, pickets ensured that there was virtually no 'blacklegging' at any of the pits, despite the often brutal attempts of the police and army to bring in 'Scab' labour.

In Glencraig, on one infamous night, the police ran amok in the streets, batoning everyone in sight, women and youngsters as well as striking miners. People were chased into houses and beaten senseless, as they tried to escape from the baton-charge.

One story has it that a young boy, who shall remain nameless, ran into a stranger's house in a state of blind terror. The woman in the house, realising the lad's plight, took the lid off the boiler and the youngster hid in there, whilst his pursuers searched in vain for him throughout the house!

Little wonder, that with such vicious steps being taken against them, some men decided to hit back. Near the end of the strike, a group of Glencraig men smashed their way into the pit and sent the cages crashing down to the bottom of the shaft, causing not inconsiderable damage. Arrests followed swiftly, many men being dragged from their beds in the middle of the night, by the police who, in several cases, had beaten in the doors of the miners' cottages.

The courts handed out severe sentences. Charlie Mitchell and Peter Aird, both members of the Communist Party, were given long prison sentences, as were Jock Mellon and Geordie 'Cooper' Armstrong, who each received twelve months imprisonment. 'Gunner Hunter', Jim and Gus Keicher, Doug Fraser and Bob Scotland were sent to jail for nine months and others were sentenced to fourteen days, or fined, or in some cases, both, as the authorities, determined to make examples of them. All told 20 men were the victims of 'British Justice'.

Whilst the '26 Miners strike was at its height, the Strike Committee did all in their power to ease the suffering of the families caught up in the strike. Soup Kitchens were opened, as one veteran recalls;

"I remember the soup kitchen at school, and how I, and my pals, received our tea, soup, or whatever, in a 2 lb. earthenware jam jar. Later on a supply of white bowls was brought to the soup kitchen, allowing us the opportunity to exchange the jam jar for a halfpenny. I can't recall the menu ever changing; soup and rice at dinner time, tea and a roll (supplied by the D.C.I.) for breakfast".

1926 Strikers Medal

Soup Kitchen, 1926 Strike

Again to provide heat at home, many miners went to an old bing from the workings of redundant Rosewell Colliery, known locally at the time, along with the few houses close by, as 'Finn-me-oot'. With pick and shovel the men would work all day, digging out a deep crater in their search for small bits of coal, sometimes taking the better part of a day just to fill a small bag. Over sixty five years later, these craters are still to be seen on the, now grass-covered bing, a lasting memento to those desperate days.

Pit Papers

The strikers organised their own papers, of which there were several different issues printed. One of these, distributed in the Glencraig and Lochore area, was entitled the 'Crow Picker', in reference to Glencraig Colliery's manager, Andrew Crowe, a man not always popular with his employees! One issue carried two roughly-sketched drawings; the first depicted two miners in the pit desperately trying to get a pit pony onto his feet. The caption underneath had one of the miners saying *"Oh God! Here comes Andrew Crowe!"* and in the second sketch *"the pony has miraculously leapt to its feet!"* A humorous example of how the men at Glencraig felt about their manager, no doubt!

Other pit papers were being printed and issued throughout Fife during the strike. The Fife District Strike Committee helped distribute at least eight such papers. The majority of which continued to be published long after the men returned to work. How many people now will remember those titles? 'The Spark', 'The Flame', 'The Lamp', 'The Panbolt', 'The Mash', and others, with more politically motivated titles — 'The Red Guard', 'The Bomb', or 'The Double Unit'.

The Pit Papers kept morale high, at a time when the Mine owners, with the full backing of the government, were using every method at their disposal to break the will of the strikers and their families. During the weeks and months of the strike, funds were raised in a variety of ways. Pipe Bands from the area on strike, played to audiences far afield in order to raise money for the strike fund, even travelling to Ireland, where they were warmly welcomed and their efforts rewarded.

There are many stories concerning the Strike, some of which, through the passage of time, have become almost legends in local mining folklore. One such story concerns the exploits of a 'mystery' man — one of the strikers — known only by his nickname, the 'Grey Seal'.

'Grey Seal' caused the police and pit officials no end of trouble. Tales of his exploits were often relayed by the older lads in the village to the youngsters, who listened wide eyed with admiration, completely enthralled by stories of yet another daring episode in the legend of this man. No doubt the older boys embellished their stories adding myth to bare facts, but, to the youngsters, Grey Seal was held in awe. He was regarded as a modern-day Robin Hood, whilst those who sought him — the police and soldiers etc. — were looked on as being the foot soldiers of the wicked Sheriff of Nottingham (in the guise of the Authorities).

Even today, 'Grey Seal's' true identity remains shrouded in mystery, known only to a few old men who are still, sixty or so years on, reluctant to reveal his real name. At the time of the Strike this secrecy was understandable. The police took the stories of 'Grey Seal' very seriously indeed, and certainly would have been highly delighted to have the mystery man in their clutches. Of course they never did manage this. It seems that those few who guard the secret of 'Grey Seal's' identity still prefer to let it remain a mystery, after all this time.

And, maybe that's as it should be.

Political Effects

The Communist Party, which had previously enjoyed considerable support amongst the villages and towns of Fife, also worked long and hard for the miners cause. The year before, Abe Moffat had been elected as a Communist on to the Parish Council at Ballingry, and at nearby Lumphinnans his brothers Jimmy and Alex were both active party members.

Membership of the Party grew, thanks largely to the efforts of local activists, such as Pat Connelly of Lochore and Bruce Wallace who would eventually become the first Communist County Councillor in Fife, elected in 1928 representing the Lumphinnans-Glencraig constituency. Wallace was one of a number of men who found himself blacklisted from the pits after the strike, and in the end had to leave the district to find work elsewhere. His seat on the County Council was taken over by Alex Moffat some years later.

Alex brother, Abe, by all accounts was almost single-handedly responsible for averting another riot in the streets of Glencraig the night after the police had baton-charged the residents there. An eye-witness account of the incident recalls

". . . Word was sent in to us that an ugly situation had developed at Glencraig

Colliery, in which men and women were facing rows of policemen.

...A group of us went down to the pit and it certainly was a tense situation when we arrived. There were two rows of police drawn up facing men and women, within about six feet of one another, the police with their batons out and the men armed with all kinds of improvised implements. Neither side would turn or give in to the other. It certainly looked like an ugly situation. After consultation, we said to the police

'Look, we better get this thing calmed down'. You behave yourselves and we'll get these lads away'.

I remember **Abe Moffat** addressing the men and saying

"All right, lads, keep facing the way you are, but when I say "one!" you take one step backward; when I say "two!" you take another step'. ....and we did that, with Abe and the leadership standing in the gap between the police and the local people until we got sufficient space between them to say 'Alright, now we can break off"'.

In the history of the trade union movement in this country, Abe Moffat's name has a special place. A man who fought courageously and gave of his best on behalf of working men and women, not just in the mining industry, but in all walks of life.

Born into a mining family in Lumphinnans in 1896, Abe himself first went to work in the pit when he was only fourteen years old, and soon became involved in the work of the trade unions. When war broke out in 1914, he enlisted in the army, even though, as a miner, military service was not compulsory. The Great War was to change Abe Moffat's political outlook forever. The government's claims that the war was being fought to create 'a land fit for heroes' did not match up to the harsh realities of life in a mining community, as Abe saw it.

Politically active throughout the 1921 strike and the intervening years, the Moffat family were 'marked men' in the eyes of the coal bosses, and when the '26 strike came to an end the entire family found themselves victimised — all the brothers were barred from working in the pits.

However, the local miners chose Abe Moffat to be their Workmen's Safety Inspector, and, despite the efforts of the mine owners to prevent him taking up this position (at one point they brought the police in to stop him from going down the mines) Abe carried out his new duties with his customary dedication to the men's cause.

In his book 'My Life with the Miners', **Abe** describes one of his many clashes with the management at Glencraig Colliery,

"... The Colliery tried another scheme to prevent us holding pit meetings. Jimmy Stewart and I went down to address a meeting of the night shift.

The Coal Company had what they called a pit policeman, who was a retired constable. On this occasion he was very pleasant to Stewart and me, but at the same time he was dressed in oil-skins. We thought there was something wrong when he was so pleasant to us, but we had no idea what the oil-skins were for. The meeting was not long started, however, when we got to know the reason. The management had fixed a water hose from the winding engine house, and the idea was that when the meeting started the hose would be put on Stewart and me. However, the plan did not work out, because instead of the stream of water going on us, it struck the policeman right between the eyes. So that ended the water hose, and we were allowed to address the meetings in peace in the future — of course, with the presence of one or two policemen to see that we did no damage to the premises".

Clearly Abe and his brother Alex were outstanding figures in the miners struggles of that day, both went on to be County Councillors as well, and indeed Alex succeeded Abe as President of the Scottish Miners Union.

However, in 1926 after nine days which shook Britain with the General Strike, the miners were left to fight on alone. After seven long months of bitter struggle, hunger and poverty, they were forced back to work, defeated, divided and demoralised, to worse conditions than before. They had lost a bitter battle against the coalowners and the Government and for ten years after, conditions in the coalfield steadily worsened, with longer hours, lower wages, harder toil, combined with unemployment and widespread malnutrition to lower the miners' standard of living.

But another consequence of both the 1921 and 1926 strikes, which was particularly pronounced in the mining villages of West Fife was the further development of a socialist tradition, which found its expression in widespread support for the Communist Party, with Glencraig returning a Communist Councillor, Bruce Wallace, in 1928 and culminating in the election of the first Communist M.P. in Britain, in 1935, the legendary Willie Gallacher.

· CHAPTER 5 ·

Childhood Memories

Whilst all the struggle and strife described in the previous chapter was going on it is interesting to examine how everyday life appeared to a young boy who grew up in the Milton Rows in Crosshill during the '20s.

This contribution from **James Rowan**:-

Memories of the Milton Rows 1919—1928

One fond memory, as a boy on the Milton, was when the Sabbath day fell. There in the morning my mother would watch us dress ourselves, in our 'Sunday best', at least to the best of her financial ability.

I can recall being fitted out in a lovely 'pepper n' salt' woollen jersey, with a collar and three buttons down the front. I can recall these jerseys were supplied by a Mr Ferguson, who gave 'credit' and who, I believe, had a small knitting business, somewhere around the Border counties. Then off to Mass, where on return, the jersey was immediately removed and laid away till the following Sunday.

There seemed at that time to be something extra special about the Sabbath, something you used to sense and feel, a serenity, and stillness, that I could appreciate but not understand. It was years later before I realised, that this was due to all the pits surrounding us, being closed on Sunday, no great chimney stack, belching out their filthy smoke and soot; no earsplitting roar from machinery, as metal ground against metal, and no loud screeching sound, from the winding engine, as it plunged the cages up and down the pit shaft.

In the autumn, going to the whinney rise in the centre of the golf course, and burning the whins, so as to find lost golf balls, then taking those that we found to the two sons of Melville the tailor, and there receiving, one penny or two pence per ball, depending on their condition.

This was on Ballingry's nine hole golf course, which was within the boundaries of the mineral railway line, Torres Loan and the Milton and Lower Milton Farm. I remember the first tee, played off the top of the Milton bing, behind the old St Kenneth's school, many of the players were local businessmen, such as Robertson — newsagent, Melville — tailor, McLeod — joinery, Haliday — Post Office, among some of the local miners I remember were, John Steel and the Morris brothers.

I remember the tall distinguished figure of Dr Sinclair, as he cycled his rounds on his all black upright bike, this my father eventually fell heir to. Father Mullheron and the Rev. Charles Mason, both of whom, I held in great awe. A wee man nicknamed 'Bash the Pan' who used to come round ringing the bell and announcing meetings etc., that were about to be held in the village.

Pug Jock, with his big flouncy bonnet, and the two long fangs, that showed when he laughed, Jock collected rags, giving us a stick of thin rock in return, his photograph hangs for posterity in the Meadows Centre.

'Kate the Tink', old Kate Cameron, who came round with her clan, mostly selling tin articles, and how we used to walk behind them, down the rows, shouting, *"A Roaster or a Toaster, or a Tinny for the wean"*.

Another personality of that time was, old 'Darkie' Blyth, who had delivered most of us when born. A stout lady, with a mop of white curly hair, framing a dark, always smiling face. I was always very impressed with her lovely little home in Park Street, shining like a new pin, and in pride of place, in the centre of her sideboard, a miniature Statue of Liberty stood.

I remember the old lady with the large gold earrings, who 'read the cups' which everyone seemed to take, oh so very seriously. We were always chased out when these 'readings' took place in our home, yet one day I crept back in. They were so intent on listening, they didn't notice me sit down in a corner, anyhow, it was my mother, and Mrs Finnerty, the one-armed postman's wife, who were having their 'cups read'. I listened intently as the old lady reeled off, what I suppose now was, a well rehearsed line, such as, *"I see a seven here, and a horse"*, etc, I recall later studying those cups, and being duly impressed, as try as I might, I could only see a mass of tea leaves, and thought she must be a very clever person indeed. I remember going outside, looking up at the sky, longing for the black cloud to pass, and bring us good fortune.

Our gas was supplied by Lochgelly Gas Coy. I can still remember the excitement and feeling of anticipation when the call went up, *"Here's the gas lassies"*, and how I would stare wide eyed, as they unlocked the cash box on the meter, and poured a large pile of pennies, placing them in piles of twelve (one shilling). It was also a red letter day for my mother, as she received a discount, or dividend, on the money collected.

I have spoken at length on some of the people, personalities and characters, who at that time, strode the 'Milton'. But what of the 'Rows' themselves. Well the Milton consisted of twenty four 'but 'n bens', laid down in two separate rows of twelve houses, and were owned by Wilson and Clyde Coal Company. Each house consisted of two rooms, and an entrance by one door only, set at ground level, with a dirt road leading right up to this doorway, so grit was carried continuously into the house, on everyones feet, during wet weather. It was difficult to determine where the road finished and the floor began.

The front room or 'kitchen' as it was called, contained two beds, set into a walled recess. The beds consisted of a rough wooden frame, on top of which lay wooden planks, this was then covered by a 'straw mattress' which, as the name implies, were wheat stalks packed tightly into a large jute bag. 'Ben the room' was another similar recessed bed. These beds were usually three to four feet above the floor level, and underneath some were stored things, such as, the cradle and the large zinc bath which was an important part of every home.

Above the fireplace, was a swan necked brass fitting, with a single gas mantle. This was the only source of light for the house. The fireplace itself was a deep recess approximately four foot high and four foot wide and two foot nine inches deep. Into this were built bricks at either side, about two foot high, and fourteen inches wide, with a heavy iron grill embedded into the brick work, and inside this a coal fire was contained, on the brickwork either side, sat the iron kettle, pots and pans.

The 'kitchen' also contained a cupboard, or what was then called a 'press' and reached almost from floor to ceiling. It was around eighteen inches deep, and contained shelves. On the bottom was the inevitable meter, in which you placed the 'penny for the gas'. The other shelves contained pots and pans etc., and above that all the dishes were stored. This completed all the facilities such a house had to offer.

Into these three beds all the family were packed, often three at the top, one at the bottom. It's beyond comprehension just to imagine, how a large family of grown-ups managed to cope; at least we were all kids when we lived in the Milton.

All the cooking and boiling of water was done on the open fire, the water being brought in from the outside well, which served the twelve families in the row. Luckily it was outside our door, as we stayed in No. 1.

Now the cooking of everything on an open fire meant that pots and pans were constantly coated with soot and tar like substances, and I can remember as a boy of seven or so outside at the well, scraping this coating off with a knife, then pulling a grass divot, wetting it at the well and scouring outside and inside of the pots with it. This was the accepted methods used to clean cooking utensils. The 'Vims' and 'Panshine's' of those days cost money, and it was a common sight, at given times of the day, to see a group of housewives, and children, all carrying out, this self same operation at the well.

Between the two rows of houses, stood the 'dry middens', where all the human excrement used to pile up, and then once a fortnight the 'scaffie' would arrive and shovel this filthy evil smelling mound into his ash cart to drive it away. In the summer months, swarms of flies and bluebottles would alight on these putrid piles and lustily and noisily feed from it, then as if by some silent signal they would all arise, and swarm through every open door in the row. But at the height of summer, we would purchase a 'fly catcher'. This was pinned to the ceiling, it was 2 foot long and 2 inches broad, covered in a dark brown sticky substance, impregnated with poison. After two, maybe three, days, this became a solid mass of dead and dying flies. I can remember looking up and often thinking how much they resembled blackcurrants.

I often look back and marvel as to how we survived such conditions, surely I and those before me, must have developed or evolved an inbuilt immunity to much of the disease of that era. I wonder how long an infant of today could survive in such an environment.

Every day, that is when my father was in work, the zinc bath was pulled from under the bed. This was filled with water, boiled on the open fire, and with only the white of his eyes showing through the grime and coal dust, he would strip to his waist, kneel down and wash in front of the fire. That is with the exception of his back. Miners have a strong superstition, that to wash the back would weaken it, so my mother, with a piece of dry rough towelling material, would vigorously rub my fathers back to remove the coal dust. The moleskin

Washing Day

trousers were dried in front of the fire. When dry, the moleskin was as stiff as a board. They were then taken outside, the solid dirt was scraped off with a knife, then beaten hard against the side of the house. This seemed to soften them, and they were washed every weekend.

All miners wore a 'peeweep'. This was a singlet or vest, either black or navy blue. This was washed every day, as were the scraping of the pit boots a daily routine. I often wondered how the woman of the house, with maybe a husband and two or three sons coming in from the pits, managed to cope, especially when you consider the inadequate facilities available.

The decorating of the home was always a limited effort due to lack of money. The ceiling always appeared patchy and lumpy. This was due to the fact that parts of the ceiling repeatedly fell down covering the whole house in a heavy layer of white dust and was invariably repaired with a different composition of lime. When decorating a packet of whitening was purchased, mixed in a pail of cold water then brushed onto the ceiling. It dried immediately, being sucked in by the lime. Wallpapers then, as can be appreciated, showed completely different designs and being the cheapest of the cheap were of very poor quality, easily torn or damaged, and it always seemed to me when pasted to the walls, to be covered in blisters and bumps.

The floor was covered with linoleum, usually of different design and age, for when the part where most of the walking took place wore out first. A portion of lino would be bought after much haggling and bargaining with the tinkers who came around in those days. The lino would then be laid on the floor then cut around and the worn part was then removed. The fact it was of a completely different design was not important, so long as it covered the bare wooden boards.

Carpeting in those early days was virtually unknown. A 'rag' rug at the fireplace was suffice, but perhaps I should explain how the 'rag' rug was made. A very large hemp or jute empty sugar bag was purchased for two pence from Paton's Turpie's shop and cut open. Then all the old woollen jerseys and cardigans, old tweed or any other cloth material, trousers, skirts, coats etc., were cut into lengths one inch wide and three inches long. Next, each of us old enough were given a wooden clothes peg with one leg broken off and the remaining leg sharpened to a point. With this pointed peg we pierced two holes in the sacking about an inch apart, pushed the three inch piece of material through from what was to be the underside of the rug, then a knot was tied on the top side, leaving two tails. The procedure was carried on until all the sacking was covered and hidden. The fact that it was a chaotic mixture of colour and material was of no importance. It was functional, warm and soft to sit on, unlike the cold hard lino.

Along one wall stood the sideboard with its mirrors, drawers and cupboards, always the largest and the main piece of furnishing in the home. In the centre of the livingroom-cum-bedroom-cum-kitchenette stood a large rectangular table, the top being of bare white wood, and occasionally, it would be covered with oilcloth. It was surrounded by four chairs, on its surface all meals were prepared and eaten, clothes were ironed, wallpaper pasted, and games such as Ludo and Snakes and Ladders were played.

Along the front of the hearth was the fender stool, made from two planks of wood, between four and five foot long, and ten inches broad, simply nailed together at right angles, and covered with a piece of lino. On this we children, sat, keeping warm during the long winter nights. The small wooden cradle seemed to be permanently at the side of the fireplace, filled with yet another young brother or sister, before the older child was ready to vacate it.

Around 1926 we were 'modernised'. A deep sink and a brass cold water tap was installed at the window, outside the house they built a W.C. I remember how narrow and confined it was. I doubt if it was as spacious as a telephone kiosk.

One of my special memories is of my mother purchasing a large chest of drawers, 'for ben the room'. I believe it was from a firm called Grubb. I clearly remember it cost £12/15/6, for I thought at the time, we would probably spend the rest of our lives, paying off this great financial burden. The reason I mentioned the chest of drawers, was because, when we lived above the Post Office in Glencraig, I remember this same chest of drawers stood against the dividing wall of the two recessed beds and there on top of it, sat in all its tangible glory our very first sign of opulence and luxury, a 'Wireless Set'. Oh what pleasure and enjoyment we derived from sitting there listening, enthralled by the music of such as Henry Hall, Ambrose, Geraldo, Lew Stone, Joe Loss and many others. Even the advent of television could never surpass the joy and magic of those early days of radio.

Those of a younger generation, who read this account of life in the 'twenties', may assume that mine was an unhappy, even unbearable, childhood. Nothing could be further from the truth. I can say with sincerity that the part of my life spent living in the 'Milton', was by far, the happiest time of all. Poverty is relative, so how could I possibly be aware of the deprivation surrounding me on every side. After all, every child in the rows was no better, nor worse, than myself. We all simply assumed this was how life was meant to be and we were completely content with that assumption''.

Where! — Oh Where

Where are the 'Raws'? — the old 'But and Ben'
Where's the barefooted, — the 'Hide and Seek' den.
Where are the tinkers, — who peddled their wares,
Where's the lamplighter — who ignited the flares.
Where are the mothers — with babes in the shawl,
Where's the old wooden cradle — the beds in the wall.
Where are the Rounders — the bat and the ball,
Where is the 'Leave O' — the 'I spy You' call
Where's the Musselburgh Fishwife — with creel on her head.
Or the horse-drawn hearse — to bury the dead.
Where is the tramcar — its loud clanging bell
The wash-house, The Midden — the old village well
Where is the wringer — the tub, and tub stool
The old leather belt — we got at the school.
Where's the horse and it's cart — the solid tyred car.
The old silent pictures — we watched at the 'Star'.
Where is the Palais — the old 'Happyland'
The Saturday night dancing — to Jack Cunningham's Band.
Where are the old names — we once knew so well,
Like Maggie, and Mary — and Katie and Nell,
Where are the Ecks — the Tams we once knew,
The Wullies, the Dods — the Jocks and the Hughs
And where are our hearts — if we ever forget
The moleskin clad miner — all coal-dust and sweat,
For he is our roots — our life, our seed-corn,
And the God Given Reason — our village was born.

J. Rowan, Lochore.

49

Local Pastimes And Games

Whilst we will deal more fully with the recognised sports in the villages in a latter chapter, it is worthwhile following James Rowan's recollections, at this stage, by mentioning some of the other pastimes that were popular, particularly amongst children.

At Glencraig, for instance, local characters like 'Fisher Clark', were usually to be found, whiling away an hour or two by the local burn. During the warm summer months, children of all ages would go swimming in the three man-made ducking pools — The 'Gooseberry', the 'Strawberry' and the 'Plum' ponds. The children of the villages had their own games as well. Street games, such as 'Kick the Can' or 'Hide and Seek', skipping games, and games like 'Paldie-beds' all of which had been played in the streets for generations, at least since the Victorian days, and were no doubt 'imported' to the area when the mines first brought the families of coal miners here.

Come the '20s, a lot of the 'original' children's games were still very much alive and well, certainly in this part of the country.

Playing or 'running' with a 'gird' was a favourite game, especially in the summertime. The famous 'gird' was usually a twenty-four inch hoop of metal, half an inch wide, which were propelled or 'driven' along the road by means of a 'cleek' or rod, fashioned from the same half-inch metal. Similar in size and shape to the gird, was the 'whin cutter' — the only difference being that the 'whin cutter' was formed out of inch-wide, flat metal. With their girds or whin cutters, the wee ones would run tirelessly for miles. A favourite run was to Loch Leven on a Sunday. In those days the children ran — there and back — without ever encountering a motor car.

Playing with cigarette cards — 'fag photos' — was a regular pastime. Capstan cigarettes in those days contained a free photocard. The object would be to collect most, if not all of the set, be they photographs of famous footballers, cricketers or movie stars etc. The youngsters collected as many cards as they could from any grown up who smoked, and several, innovative games were played with these prized 'Fag-photos'.

Then, as now, little girls played with their skipping ropes, or made up a 'shoppie', 'selling' old bits of junk to one another, using broken bits of crockery as their 'money'. 'Paldie-beds', or 'Ball-beds', where an old, flat tin of some sort, weighed down by being filled with sand and dirt, was shoved along the streets to a given spot, or 'Square', where it had to be retrieved either by hopping to it, or jumping over to it, was played as well.

James Rowan explains, *"None of us possessed bikes or large toys, and T.V. and Radio were still something in the future. Biscuits, cakes and fruit were non-existent in our homes, and we seldom had any money. If ten of us kids played 'Hide and Seek' for a week, you could be sure there was never one halfpenny amongst us.*

Only the penny matinee, on a Saturday, cost our parents any money, and even then, only a penny. No halfpenny for a stick of rock, or treacle toffee was ever expected. But, after the film finished we would all stream out, blinking in the strong daylight, and try to immitate our great Cowboy heroes, Tom Mix and Buck Jones, or else the swash-buckling hero Douglas Fairbanks Snr. Then, on our way home we would kill off all the 'baddies'. Those days were a heaven of make-believe, in our deprived, but totally uncomplicated young lives".

Rounders, a game similar to the American game of baseball, was played by boys and girls alike, on the drying greens where clothes poles could be used as corner markers. The boys found that the clothes poles made excellent goal posts when football was the game being played.

Bob Penman remembers making 'Fire-cans'' as a young boy.

"These were made from an old syrup or treacle tin. You punched holes in the bottom with a nail and then, using a tin opener, made six or more slits down the sides of the can, from top to bottom. Once this was done, a wire handle was attached and a fire was lit inside the tin. To keep the 'fire-can' lit, you had to swing it round and round in circles.

Other games that come to mind are 'Bools' — Marbles — which was a fairly seasonal game, 'Leave O' and 'Tag' which were played by girls as well as boys and 'Cock a Dunty'. Girls and boys used to organise concerts in the Rows. Not many people had wireless sets and so the summer concerts were a great form of entertainment during the school holidays''.

Continued Expansion Of The Village

Despite the obvious levels of poverty brought about, mainly by the poor wages and the constant threats of lay-offs and redundancies that existed at that time, nevertheless it is also true that the villages of Benarty did prosper, after a fashion, and continued, slowly, but surely, to expand.

Take for example, Crosshill, where in the area that is now edged by, at one end, the entrance to the Meadows Country Park, and at the other by the Benarty Tavern, there were no less than two dozen shops in the 1920s! The community was amply served by at least two Butchers' shops, a couple of Bakers' and two chip shops. There were Joiners and Ironmongers, as well as a Chemists' (Thompsons'), and an Undertakers' business, complete with horse-drawn hearse.

The 'Star' cinema, where Euphemia Rennie accompanied the silent films on the piano did a roaring trade. Euphemia gave the audience a musical soundtrack making Chaplin, Tom Mix and Rin, Tin, Tin all the more exciting*. The two Public Houses and Ex-Servicemen's club were equally busy. The Benarty Tavern opened its doors for the first time during this period, having recently been converted from a licensed Grocers' shop, owned, incidentally by the parents of Alex Robertson, who had worked in the office at the Mary Colliery before joining the army in the Great War.

There were other shops, of course. At least three clothes shops, as well as a number of small businesses that catered for a good bit of the villages needs. And of course, all else failing, there was always the 'Packie Man', ('Shilling a week man') who came around the doors, selling his wares from a suitcase, giving credit to grateful households, collecting (or not as the case may be) his shilling a week thereafter.

As a matter of interest one of the 'Packie Men' was Jack Rifkind, an ancestor of the man who became Minister of Transport, Malcolm Rifkind and is now Minister of Defence. Fair to say the Rifkind family has travelled a long way from those days!

John Duncan, the son of Glencraig Colliery's Cashier, remembers as a boy running errands to the shops at Glencraig.

"... going to the Lochgelly Cooperative Store and to David Gibson, the shoe repairer, whose workshop was originally in the Contill Row. He later shifted his business to the annex of a building on the main road. His premises used gas for lighting, and for heating the tools. I remember David Gibson well, with a mouthful of tackets which he expertly put into his miners' boots with a large flat file. Mr Gibson was an expert at his profession, and if you required new leather soles, you usually got them hand sewn. Prior to setting up on his own, David Gibson worked for the Lochgelly Co-op. He lost his only son in the Second World War".

And if the local shops weren't enough, there were larger stores, offering a greater choice of merchandise, just a tram-ride away, at Lochgelly, Cowdenbeath and Dunfermline. The trams, open to the elements as they

Footnote: * The Star Cinema finally closed in the early 1960s when the advent of television brought the demise of many small cinemas in the country.

always were, remained the most popular form of transport in the district until they were eventually replaced by the buses in the middle of the 1930s. The trams gave people access to the Railway stations, and they carried the football supporters to the bigger towns on match days. It was not unusual to see the lines of 'Special' trams, conveying large crowds to a big game at Dunfermline or Cowdenbeath, the trams running head to tail and filled to capacity. On at least one occasion the local police stopped one such tram and boarded it to count the numbers of people travelling on it. They were astonished to find no less than one hundred and thirty four people packed in to it!

People also moved house, or flitted, via the trams. It was a common sight to see rolls of linoleum, chairs and other pieces of furniture packed in to the area beside the driver, as a family took advantage of the tram to move their possessions.

As the competition from the bus companies — Peatties of Crosshill, Forresters' of Lochgelly and Scott's of Cowdenbeath, to name but a few, increased, so the demise of the trams accelerated. The buses could, and did, run in front of the trams, and pick up potential customers waiting at the recognised tram stops.

In 1935, the bus group W. Alexander, bought over the majority of shares in the Tramways, and ended the short, but glorious career, of trams in this area at least.

Two tramcars were taken to Northern Ireland and provided a service for paying customers there until at least 1949, whilst the majority of the others were to end up minus their wheels, as holiday homes at the nearby resorts of Burntisland and Kinghorn.

· CHAPTER 6 ·

The Hungry Thirties

There are some people who would argue that the 'Hungry Thirties' were merely an extension for the miners of the unemployment and poverty which characterised the 'Twenties'.

Whilst this may be debatable, official figures from that time do show a massive loss of jobs in the Industry. Of the 143,267 men employed in the Scottish coalfields in 1923, the figures had slumped to 82,358 by 1932. In effect in the mining villages at least 40% of the miners were now idle and living on 'unemployment assistance'. This was the period of the 'Means Test' when even the meagre income could be removed if the local 'dole' clerk decided that "you were not genuinely seeking work".

Rab Smith, a Lumphinnans man who became a Fife County Councillor for Lumphinnans and South Glencraig, was but one victim of the Means Test regulations. In later years he recalled how he reacted, to his cost, when confronted by an over-zealous official.

". . . the poverty that existed in this area in the thirties was terrible. I'll give you an instance. . . that I experienced myself. I was on the dole, and at that time there was a clause that was introduced by Maggie Blumfield, a Labour renegade, and that clause was 'Not genuinely looking for work'.

You had to go to the clerk when you went to sign on the dole, and tell him where you were looking for work. So, this morning I was in fine fettle. He said, "Where were you on Monday?" Says I — "Nowhere" "Tuesday?" — "Nowhere" — "Wednesday?" — "Nowhere" — "Thursday?" — "Nowhere" "Friday?" — "Nowhere" — "Saturday?" — Nowhere".

He said "Would you sign that statement?
I said "Yes, I'll sign that statement, because it's true".

So I signed the statement. I was struck off, of course: 'Not genuinely seeking work'.

I appealed against that and went to a tribunal. I lost the case, even at the tribunal. The Lawyer at the time was Currie, and he said to me, — "Smith — (you see, these fellows don't cry you by your first name — Smith, the old army style). "Smith, did you know what you were doing when you signed that statement".
"Yes, I knew what I was doing, because it was the truth".

I had tramped all over this area, as hundreds of other workers were doing, in order to find work, and we couldn't get work, and in my opinion, it's the Government's responsibility to find work for the unemployed".

The reaction to the unemployment, the poverty, evictions and the hated Means Test, was the organisation of the famous Hunger Marches.

The first such March in Fife was on the 26th January 1932, led by Alex Moffat, the Communist County Councillor who represented Glencraig. The marchers main demands were *"That the Fife County Council should not co-operate with the Means Test; its Public Assistance Committee should make up cuts in unemployment benefits; work schemes or able-bodied relief, equal to the Labour Exchange scales of benefit in September 1931 should be provided irrespective of incomes of relatives; the feeding of schoolchildren should be taken in hand; there should be a 25 per cent reduction in rents, starting with those of County Council houses; workers with less than £2.25 a week household income should be exempted from payment of rates; and no County Council official should be paid more than £600 a year".* The council agreed to remit the matter to the Public Assistance Committee.

This march was followed by another to Edinburgh, in February 1932 and over the next few years numerous marches took place throughout the County up to 1938, most of which were met by hostility on the part of the authorities. Indeed in 1934 seven West Fife Hunger Marchers were arrested on their return from London and charged by Fife County Council as Public Assistance Authority with deserting or failing to maintain their wives and children while they were away on the March.

All seven marchers pleaded not guilty at the trial at Dunfermline Sheriff Court. The prosecution dropped the charge of desertion, and the men were charged only with neglecting to maintain their wives and children. Only one case, Walter Mannarn, aged thirty-seven, of Lumphinnans, was proceeded with, to stand as a test case for the others. Mannarn was found not guilty so the other cases were abandoned.

Rab Smith was one of those who took part in the 'Hunger Marches' in the 1930s, marching to London, as was Norman Graham, who became one of the most influential and long serving members of the Fife County Council. Today's Sheltered Housing complex at Balbedie Avenue is called Graham Court, in honour of this former councillor.

Conflict At Work

For those in work, life was certainly no bed of roses either. Whilst there were no great National Strikes, such as in 1921 and 1926, there were a series of local strikes in the early '30s, against Coal Owners repeatedly attempted to cut already low wage rates. In July 1931, during one such strike at Glencraig, police were once again fighting miners in the streets of Central Fife, and on Glencraig Bridge, the striking miners managed to derail the tramcars that had been used to bus 'Blacklegs' in to work.

The following year 900 men at the Mary stayed out on strike for four weeks after the Fife Coal Company had demanded that their employees accept yet another wage cut. In both cases, the Unions succeeded in obtaining Strike Relief from the Local Authorities for the women and children, and set up communal kitchens to feed the strikers. Of great importance, the miners, for the first time got the guarantee from the Coal Owners that no victimisation would take place on the resumption of work. This was in sharp contrast to the great Strikes of '21 and '26, when scores of active and militant miners had been victimised.

Throughout the 1930s this continued to be the pattern, with a kind of guerilla warfare being conducted against the Coal owners which only came to an end with the advent of the Second World War.

Local Organisations

Nevertheless, even in the midst of all the hardship and suffering, unemployment and low wages, people did their best to carry on with their lives as normal as possible and a number of local Organisations sprung up, playing a worthwhile role in everyday life. Amongst these were various Youth Organisations.

The Boys' Brigade formed at Lochcraig church in 1934, ran a summer camp for its members and this was very much looked forward to by the boys and young lads who made up the Company.

Set up by a Mr Ritchie, the Brigade had a strength of some eighty members in its heyday. Later, Mr J. Kirk, who had been connected with the running of the Boy Scout movement since the days before the First World War, took over control of the Lochcraig Boys Brigade, and ran the company for a further thirteen years, before handing over the reins to the next Captain, Mr D. McGregor. In the years that followed, other Brigade Captains included Mr C. McLelland and Mr Finlayson, both local men.

In addition, the 20th Fife (Ballingry) Boys Scouts troop had been formed in the mid-twenties by a Mr Whitehead. They held their first meeting on the out-crop of rock, just off Ballingry Road. Around 1930 William Wilson took over the day to day running of the troop followed by Sandy Scott, who was assisted by Norman Stewart and William Justice. In 1937, Douglas Johnston and James Justice took the troop over and ran it for the next two years or so, before both men entered the Forces.

During the Second World War, the troop was more or less abandoned, at least until the latter years of the war, when Archie Park took an interest and reformed it. The 20th held many camps during the years, never costing the boys' parents any more than £1 for their children to attend. The troop would travel by train or by a Wilson and Clyde lorry driven by Hugh Begg to these summer camps, sometimes accompanied by members of one of the local pipe bands.

Catering for the female half of the young population were the Girl Guides, first formed in 1920, and ably served in the beginning by a local woman, Miss Mason. The Guides' first few meetings had to be held in the open-air, on the Clune, as no accommodation could be found for them in the district.

Under the leadership of one of the local teachers, Miss Sorrie, the Guides eventually found a meeting place within Ballingry School, before moving to a room at Crosshill School, when the next Captain, Miss Ferguson, took charge. Later Guide Leaders were Miss Bauld, Miss George and Miss Paterson.

Sadly, neither the Girl Guides nor the Scouts nor the Boys Brigade exist any longer in the district. Youngsters, for years, have had other distractions to occupy their leisure time and the need for organisations such as the Brigade and the Guides gradually dwindled. Still, even the mention of any of these institutions will, no doubt, bring to mind many fond memories for former members, wherever they may be.

Pipe Bands

At the time both Lochore and Glencraig could boast of prize-winning bands. The Lochore and Crosshill Pipe Band came into existence in 1920, under the leadership of David Storrar, the band's first Pipe-Major. That first pipe-band included four members of the Storrar family — Pipe Major, Davie, his father, Pipe Sergeant Tom Storrar, and brothers James and John amongst the ranks of pipers. Members of the band are shown in the photograph in this book.

First Lochore & Crosshill Pipe Band

Lochore & Crosshill Pipe Band

58

As a matter of record, one of the first Committees of the Lochore and Crosshill Pipe Band was made up of the following individuals: Andrew Redpath, President; James Guthrie, Secretary; Barney Fannan, Treasurer; John Quinn, James Storrar and David Storrar.

In the period of the 'Hungry Thirties' (and indeed, right up until the present day) Pipe Bands were always devising new ways to raise funds. Surely one of the most original ideas for fund-raising was the one thought up by members of the Lochore and Crosshill Band in May, 1934. The Band held a 'Bonny Baby' Show in the Mission Hall at Glencraig, and, judging by the number of entries, some 80 to 90 children, the idea was very successful in raising money for the bands upkeep. Mr William Reid, of Cowdenbeath, opened the baby show and the judges included a doctor and two nurses, all from outside the district, to ensure impartiality, no doubt!

The results were as follows:-

Age Group

Up to Six Months	1st	Hugh Lawson, 68 North Glencraig.
	2nd	Anna McCue, 24 Factory Road, Cowdenbeath.
	3rd	Alexander Harper, 70 North Glencraig.
Six Months to One Year	1st	Ina Macari, Lochore.
	2nd	John McGinley, Erin Cottage, Crosshill.
	3rd	Robert Davidson, 3 Glen Allan Street, Lochore.
One Year to Two Years	1st	Jeannie Cumming, Mannering Street, Lochore.
	2nd	David Gibb, 98 North Glencraig.
	3rd	Alexander Fernie, 44 Park Street, Crosshill.
Two Years to Three Years	1st	Daisy Seaman, 26 Montrose Crescent, Lochore.
	2nd	James King, 91 Waverly Street, Lochore.
	3rd	Anna Page, Park Avenue, Kinglassie.

It would be interesting, no doubt, to find out where all these 'Bonny Babies' are now!

Glencraig Pipe Band

Glencraig Pipe Band

The Glencraig Colliery Pipe Band was formed at about the same time as its local rival, under Pipe Major Tom Jackson, but it was not until 1932 that it took its name from the Colliery.

In the early days the Band would practice in the open air, at the Avenue leading to Glencraig House, which in those days was lined with trees, and the band must have been an impressive sight as they rehearsed for future public appearances there, before moving to premises more suitable to their needs, when a band hut was built for them. The band hut, built out of old army huts obtained, somehow, from Rosyth, stood some 500 yards south of Glencraig Bridge and close to the road known locally as 'Gordon Place'. Today, that area, like so much of the surrounding district, has been returned, once more, to grazing land.

In the period between the two World Wars, the Glencraig Colliery Pipe Band flourished considerably, winning many national and international piping events. They were runners-up to the World Champions in 1935, and in 1936 they themselves took the title. At the same time they were Fife Champions for three consecutive years. Always available for Galas and public gatherings, the Glencraig band was highly popular and enjoyed huge support for a good many years. Throughout its lifetime, the band was served admirably by many hard working and dedicated committee members, of which the following are only some:-

Owen McGuire, Sam O'Hare, Willie McLean, Dan Murphy, Mick Cooney, J. and I. Glencross (father and son), J. Hunt, J. Martin, J. Provan, J. Smith, J. Carrens and A. Moffat.

During the Second World War, many of the band's members served as pipers and drummers in the armed forces, whilst others played in the local Home Guard band. Reformed shortly after the war, the Glencraig Pipe Band soon resumed its winning ways, and by 1947 had won the coveted Cowal Championship.

To name each and every one of the band's pipers and drummers over the years would be an almost impossible task, but here, with apologies to those omitted from the list, are some of the men who brought enjoyment to many people in the early years of the band's life:—

Pipe Majors Tom and James Jackson, Alex Walkinshaw, J. Murphy and A. Hamilton.

Pipers James McInnes, (Pipe Sergeant), G. Walkinshaw, A. Clelland, J. McQuillan, J. McGuire, J. Laurie, H. McPherson, G. Murphy, A. Calder and William Marshall.

Drum Major W. Briggs, drummers D. Bauld, N. Stewart, Tom Brown, Martin Gilfeather, P. Clarke and G. Whisker.

With the eventual closure of the Colliery, lack of funding and a general dwindling of support caused the band financial and other problems. It soldiered on bravely for a few more years but today, like so many other popular 'institutions' of the past, the Glencraig Colliery Pipe Band is no longer with us, a part of our mining heritage lost forever.

Sporting Developments

The '30s saw some developments which would benefit the more sports-inclined members of the community. Lochore Welfare F.C. played its first match in 1934 and by the end of the decade could boast a £400 purpose-built pavilion as one of its assets. Ballingry Golf Club also moved into a new pavilion in 1935 and for those who enjoyed the popular pastime of cycling, the Ballingry Cycling Club ws set up in 1931.

In 1938, a local Councillor, Alex Page, secured a grant from the King George V Jubilee Trust, to establish a central playing park at Crosshill, which would serve the needs not only of residents there, but also of the people of Glencraig and Lochore.

The Churches

Religion was also an important part of people's lives, and the established Churches continued to carry out their Spiritual work. A recollection by Arthur McGachie illustrates the commitment that the Catholic community had towards their church.

At St. Kenneth's, the statues that stand on either side of the altar, came from the Roman Catholic Church at Cowie, in Stirlingshire. Their journey from Cowie to Lochore was not entirely without incident. **Arthur McGachie** vividly remembers,

"Father William McCabe told me about the two statues and how he had been offered them as a gift for St. Kenneth's. The problem was going to be getting them to Lochore.

I suggested we borrow a truck to transport them, and this we did. My brother, William, and I were just leaving to go to Stirling to collect the statues when the church gardener, Jim Moore, asked to come with us. As there wasn't any room in the cab of the truck, Jim sat up at the back of the vehicle.

Well, with the bottom of the truck covered in straw, we duly collected the statues and loaded them onto the truck. As they were inclined to roll about quite a bit, old Jim sat in the back with them, between Our Lady and the Sacred Heart.

All was fine, until we drew alongside a bus. The passengers, on looking out of the windows, saw Jim with his travelling 'companions', and soon began to take a keen interest in us. One lady even blessed herself.

I hope she is aware that we, and the statues, had a safe journey home".

However, apart from the established Churches, another religious group was formed in August 1931, when the first Gospel Hall meeting in Glencraig was held, in the Co-operative Buildings (Lofty View) adjacent to Malvenan's Bakery. To cope with increasing numbers, the group later acquired premises in Lynas Buildings and created a fine hall which could seat 150. Because of mining subsidence, they had to move once again, this time to the old billiard hall situated in the Co-operative Buildings on the Main street, remaining there until the village of Glencraig finally closed in 1967.

An interesting point of history concerns the closure of this last hall. The members of the Gospel Hall were given permission to demolish and retain the materials from the Co-operative Building, associated houses, and also Malvenan's Bakery. After a year of preparation, bricks, slates, wood and steel girders were re-used in the construction of the present Gospel Hall, Southfield Avenue, Ballingry. So part of old Glencraig is still in daily use!

Perhaps the abiding memories of this group were two-fold. Firstly, the large support given to its Sunday School work, the annual outings were huge affairs and entailed often having a train to take 250 children and parents to some seaside resort. Secondly, it conducted services in the open-air. A favourite stance was the Square, South Glencraig on a summer's evening. Crowds would often come out to listen as these local Christians would preach the Gospel. This continues to the present on the streets of Ballingry and district.

It is worth noting that, despite the variety of origins of the people who had come to work in the local pits, and their differing religions, there was little sign of the bitter conflict between them that was common in other parts of Scotland.

The absence of such conflict could be explained by the fact that the very nature of work in the pits meant that people had to co-operate, if only to survive, and this bond continued above ground. This attitude of co-operation indeed extended to the Masonic Lodge, whose premises were frequently used for all manner of functions and were denied to no one.

The Lodge itself, Ballingry 1183 was consecrated on May 24th, 1919, by the Earl of Elgin, Provincial Grand Master of Fife and Kinross. The first lodge meeting was held in the Mission Hall, Lochcraig, two days later. It had its nucleus in resident Brethern who were members mainly of the Lodge Minto-Lochgelly, Lodge Oak-Kelty and Lodge St. Fothads-Auchterderran. The Mission Hall was to be used for their meetings for the next ten years, before the Lodge moved to its own Masonic Temple on Manse Road, where a divine Service was held on June 30th, 1929.

The first office bearers were Brother William G. Graham, RWM. John C. George, John Brown, George Beattie, L. Taylor, William C. Clarke (Secretary), Robert Donaldson (Treasurer), G. Reid, James Bauld, Malcolm McCallum and John McCallum.

The premises are still used today, not only for Masonic purposes, but also they are freely available to members of the community who require them for social functions.

Holidays

It should be appreciated that, up until the days of the Second World War, the miners received no holiday pay. Indeed for seventy or so years, the Fife Miners celebrated the winning of the first 'eight-hour day' in Europe by declaring the first Monday and Tuesday in June to be Miners' holidays but although called 'holidays', these two days were, in effect, two idle days, as no work meant no pay — holiday or not! This applied also for the annual holiday week, traditionally taken in July, and New Year's day if it happened to fall on a working day.

So in the 1930s, when money was scarce, and idle days were many, the annual summer holiday was very different from those enjoyed by most people today. **James Spence**, a young boy in those pre-war days, remembers vividly how those annual holidays were celebrated.

"In the days before the Second World War, the miners broke off on the Saturday for their week's holiday, with one week's pay to keep them for a fortnight. The holiday week was looked on as idle time. On those days you did not go far — if you were lucky you might go to Burntisland, or Kinghorn, for a day at the seaside.

The road from Lochore to Loch Leven would often be thronged with people going to and coming from the Loch. In those days, of course, you had to walk there, and back. The shores of the Loch would be black with people! Some of the miners who were lucky enough to own a bicycle, would be seen heading in the direction of Glendevon, with their tent and trusty frying pan tied to the back of the bike, a fishing rod strapped onto the bar.

Of course, some men never got any further than the pub! There, they drank to their hearts' content for the first few days until their money ran out, and left them with nothing but long faces for the rest of the week.

Later, just before the outbreak of war in 1939, a form of holiday pay was introduced. This did ease the money problems slightly, but due to the travel restrictions imposed during war-time, the pattern of holidays was much the same as in those pre-war days".

Gala Days

For youngsters and adults alike, there was always the Gala Days to look forward to, and this was certainly the most popular period for these colourful and happy events. Races were run, and the local pipe bands, always popular and well supported, brought the crowds out in droves on Gala days!

On such days, the drone of the pipes would provide a colourful background accompaniment to the highland dancing and the children's races, which at times, could be seen as little more than organised chaos, with infants straying on to the running track from time to time, and mothers hurriedly retrieving them before they were trampled underfoot by the enthusiastic competitors. Some of the children used to steal away before the races, to 'practice' for their events, returning bright eyed and full of confidence, only to be well beaten in the race itself and face the barracking and jibes of their friends afterwards.

For all the kids, whether they were participating in the races or not, there was the picnic to look forward to. There, they would get their bottle of lemonade and bag of buns, the lemonade being guzzled down at speed, in an effort to get the penny return on the empty bottle!

And so the Gala day would continue, a day of racing and chasing, and pipe bands and parades, and dancers, until eventually all would head for home, tired out but totally satisfied.

At Glencraig in the twenties, no Gala was complete without big Geordie Morris leading the parade. Big Geordie was mentally handicapped, unable to communicate properly due to a bad speech impediment, and because of this, his life was often made a misery by the local men and lads, who would constantly goad him. Unable to answer back properly, big Geordie would roar at them and frantically wave his arms about, much to the men's amusement, until the big man's mother, a little white-haired old lady, would come over, and speak soft words of encouragement to Geordie, calm the lad down and lead him back to the house.

But, come the children's Gala day, Geordie Morris came into his own. On those days he was king of the village, the happiest man in Glencraig, as he strutted and marched right at the front of the pipe band, like a king leading his army, as the parade wound its way through the village streets. On it went, until with big Geordie at its head, and all the children following on, the parade reached Bore Park, the venue for the day's entertainments. In a life that could not have been in any way described as a happy one, surely the gala days must have been Geordie Morris' greatest hours.

Other Local Characters

Glencraig, of course, had a number of other characters who were remembered for many years and are still talked about. **James Rowan** recalls some of those who impressed him during the Thirties

"Of all the characters I knew, I envied none more than Old Peter Campbell,

whose whole attitude to life, and living, seemed to manifest and project peace and tranquillity. 'Old Peter', who I would pass each day, as I cut across, past his 'hen run', sitting on a rough made form, contentedly, smoking his old black pipe and watching for hours, his beloved hens. Because of a badly mutilated hand, he was on constant night shift underground, watching a fan or pump, which entitled Peter to work weekends. His life, it always seemed to me, was split evenly, between his work, and his hens, and bantams.

Another old character, in the village of Glencraig, who I had an awful lot of time and respect for, was old Frankie Gibb, a conscientious and hard working member of the community. Frankie employed by the Wilson and Clyde Coal Company, as a sort of handy man, carrying out small maintenance jobs on the miners homes, such as replacing slates on the roof etc. He also swept 'lums' as a sideline. It always seemed to me, that Frankie, was perpetually in working clothes. I can only picture him with a large smile on his soot-blackened face, and one strap of his overalls, continuously waving in the wind, a cheery and very obliging soul!

I can picture too Old Johnny Layden with his walrus moustache, and shiny rosy cheeks, that belied his age. Johnny, in his middle seventies, could kick his own height, or near enough. Always attired in his worn, but neat, navy blue suit and black muffler, and a pair of sturdy black boots, that always seemed to shine, like ebony. Johnny was always agonisingly slow and correct, in everything he seemed to do, or say.

Then, of course, 'Bump' Holland, who had played the big drum in the pipe band. Everyone knew 'Bump', the complete extrovert. He just had to be always in the limelight, grinning, and dispensing his pawkey humour. My own opinion of Bump — a lovable rogue".

Looking back on these characters and organisations and seeing how people lived their lives it is clear that through the 1930's, despite the present hardship and poverty in the villages, a spirit of community prevailed, and a hope that the future could only be better. This proved to be wishful thinking, because the decade, which had begun with the Wall Street crash, was to end with another World War.

Prelude To War

As the 1930s drew to a close, the storm clouds of war were gathering over Europe, as Germany prepared to re-draw the map of the world by military action. The prelude was to be the Spanish Civil War, in which the Germans and Italians would be able to test the aircraft and weapons they would eventually use against the Allies, in support of General Franco, who had led an insurrection against the democratically elected Spanish Government.

Willie Gallacher, the Communist M.P. for West Fife went to Spain as a special correspondent for the Daily Worker, and his commitment to the Spanish people was a major factor in influencing hundreds of men and women to go from this country as volunteers in the International Brigade. As part of the British battalion 38 men and women from Fife went to Spain, including three from Glencraig, Tom Howie, J. McCormack and 'Chick' McCormack.

From Spain, in 1937, **Chick** wrote to his parents the following:

". . . the Spanish people are the kindest and bravest people I have met. The stories about them looting the churches are all lies. Any damage that has been done has been caused by bombs and shells. This proves to anyone that the loyalists are very honest and just. The Rebels are a brutal mob. They say theirs is a 'Christian Front' — yet they use 'dum-dum' and explosive bullets. They shoot our Red Cross men when they go out to bring in our wounded and dead comrades. This proves they do not understand the word 'Christian'. . . "

Despite their own poverty, many people donated to 'Aid for Spain', All over Britain people organised events to raise money, and in Lochore, the Masonic Hall was regularly used by the local branch of the Co-operative Guild for that purpose. **Rab Smith**, the Councillor, often spoke later of another fund-raising enterprise.

". . . I remember at that time we sold a cigarette called 'Smoke Clouds'. We sold them in order to raise money to send to the Spanish Aid Fund. I'm sure they injured the health of some of the people who smoked them, because they had a terrible smell!

Nevertheless, I wasn't concerned, because I was a non-smoker, and I wasn't concerned about people's health. I was concerned about saving Britain and saving the people in Spain".

The Spanish Civil war dragged on until March 1938, but the International Brigade had been withdrawn the previous September, and the Fife men returned to a hero's welcome. With the Spanish capital Madrid falling to General Franco, the Republican government had been defeated, and it was clear that the Second World War was only a matter of months away.

Memory Lane

*Mary
Colliery
Miners*

*Glencraig
Colliery
Miners*

*Glencraig
Blacksmiths*

Memory Lane

*Mary
Colliery
Football
Team*

*Glencraig
Colliery
Football
Team*

*Mines
Rescue
Team*

CHAPTER 7

Once More At War

On Sunday, September 3rd, 1939, millions of people across the British Isles tuned in their radio sets to hear Prime Minister Neville Chamberlain address the nation. His broadcast was brief. Once more, Great Britain was at war with Germany and her allies, in Europe and elsewhere.

To the majority, the news, as dreadful as it was, came as no surprise. Tension had been building in Europe ever since Adolf Hitler had come to power in Germany in the early 1930s, and the reluctance of the British and French Governments to take action against the other European dictators in the following years had made the present situation inevitable. The Munich agreement of 1938 — Chamberlain's 'Peace In Our Time' plea — now lay in tatters as Hitler's armies marched across the continent, invading nation after nation. Finally, when Poland fell in early September, the crisis came to a head.

In reality, preparations for the defence of Britain had been started months before. Early in 1939, as the threat of war became imminent and the government began to be concerned about the possibility of attack from the skies, the Air Raid Precautions (the A.R.P.) which later became know as the Civil Defence Volunteers, was formed.

Crosshill Fire Brigade

Six Air Raid Wardens' posts were installed in the Benarty area. These purpose-built posts — made entirely of brick, with a concrete roof, and completely devoid of windows — could easily accommodate a team of up to eight Wardens at one time. Under the command of Chief Warden William Wilson, who set up a Headquarters in Crosshill School, the local warden's posts were situated throughout the district. Glencraig had two posts, yet another was located at the quarry at Lochcraig, and Crosshill had one as well. The old Miners' Institute at Lochore was the site of another building, whilst the area's sixth post was at Ballingry School. In addition to the A.R.P. squads, there was a Rescue Service, led by Mr. Archie Russell. Stationed at Farmers' Yard on Park Street, the Rescue Service were given the use of one of Farmers' lorries to carry their equipment, as and when needed.

With the threat of Air Raids came the very real possibility of fire, brought on by the enemy's incendiary bombs. With this in mind, a local Fire Service was organised at Crosshill. Led by Charles Smith, the fire service boasted a crew of six full-time firemen and twenty four volunteers who worked on a part-time basis. The squad used an old taxi to pull their mobile pump. Local history relates, sadly, that, resplendent in their Fire-fighters' uniforms as the men might have been, the only time they were called to deal with a fire was when their own Fire Station was set alight, whilst they held a dance in one of the local halls! Crosshill School became the home of the First Aid Unit, under the guiding hand of Robert Graham.

Finally, the district had its own Communication Service network. Volunteers relayed messages between the various posts and Civil Defence H.Q.s. Bearing in mind that, at that time, very few public buildings, to say nothing of private dwellings, had telephones, the men and women of the Communication Service, who went from post to post, either on bicycle, or on foot, certainly 'did their bit' for the war effort.

The Black Out

As soon as war was declared a 'Black Out' was imposed, in order to make it difficult for enemy aircraft to pinpoint targets, be they military or civilian. The first visible signs of the war came to the district with the repainting of all the lamp posts in the village streets. The normally dark green paintwork was hastily covered with a coat of silver paint in order for them to be seen more easily in the black out. Nevertheless, a journey at night, no matter how short, must have been quite an endurance test in the dark of a black out evening. To make matters worse, all sign posts and street signs were removed. Little wonder then, that by far the most common injuries that the First Aid Units had to deal with were caused by people walking into walls (and silver lamp posts!) etc. during the course of an evening!

Local school teacher, **Mrs Ada Halliday** remembers the black out well, *"...you had to have any lights in your house completely blacked out from view from outside. In addition, the street lights were switched off, and if you used a torch, you had to cover the lamp part with a piece of paper to diffuse the torch's beam.*

One evening I went outside, perhaps I was just making sure that all my curtains were tightly drawn, I'm not sure now. Anyway, I bumped into someone, and immediately put the light on to see who it was. It was the local police sergeant and he was not at all pleased with me!

He told me in no uncertain terms to watch what I was doing and, 'Put that light out! 'As I say he was not at all pleased. In the black out it was quite common to walk into lamp posts in the dark! That was just one of the hazards of life then. People simply didn't go out at night if they could help it".

The civilian population were issued with Gas Masks. Cumbersome and restrictive as these were, everyone had to carry their gas mask wherever they went, especially in the early days of the war, when the horrific reminders of the mustard gas effects in the First War were to be seen in the ex-soldiers' who had been gassed at the front. Outside the wardens' buildings, large flat boards, painted with a special substance, which would change colour if in contact with poison gas, were positioned so that all could see them and take the appropriate action.

People everywhere began to dig Air Raid shelters, although it has to be said, few were ever completed. On the day war was declared, there was an Air Raid alert sounded, but thankfully, on this occasion, it turned out to be a false alarm. However, a few weeks later, there was a daylight raid on the River Forth and an attempt was made to bomb the railway bridge there. Many local people will remember that raid, as a number of German 'planes flew over the area, dodging the Anti-Aircraft Guns, on their run to the Bridge. Fortunately, the raid was unsuccessful and the Rail Bridge remained intact.

Between 1940 and 1942, there were considerable enemy activity over Fife, mostly single night time raids where lone aircraft would fly over the area, dropping bombs indiscriminately, thankfully doing little or no damage. The Scotlandwell to Ballingry road was hit and damaged by a stray bomb, while on yet another raid, this time at night, a single aircraft, coming from the direction of Rosyth Dockyard and heading towards the sea, released its load of incendiary bombs over Lochore. Whether the pilot had aimed for the village or not, will never be known, but his bombs landed on the ground where the Opencast washers now stand. The site of the present day opencast mine was also hit that night by at least three high explosive devices.

At every raid the noise of the aircraft was mingled with the sounds of anti-aircraft guns and the glare of the search lights in the night sky. The nearest Gun emplacement to Glencraig and Lochore was situated at the 'Jeltex' factory at nearby Halbeath. At the height of the 'blitz', the anti-aircraft guns and the men and women who operated them were kept very busy indeed.

For a while there was a searchlight unit stationed at Ballingry, opposite the avenue. Later on it was moved to the top of Dunmore Hill and finally it went to the Hill Road. On several nights during the concentrated raids on Clydeside, the sky above Lochoreshire was filled with hundreds of enemy aircraft making their way across country. On those nights there was intense gunfire and the searchlights lit the sky.

T h e   L . D . V .

With the ever increasing possibility of invasion, especially in the weeks after Dunkirk, local armed units were set up as a last line of defence. Formed initially as the Local Defence Volunteers (L.D.V.), or as they were quickly nicknamed, 'Look, Duck and Vanish'. These units soon became known as the Home Guard.

At first they trained with broomsticks (no guns available for them) in the playground at Crosshill school, but later on, under the command of Major Hunter, the Home Guard took over the Mission Hall (Eastern Star) in Crosshill and, with their new issue of uniforms and (at long last) rifles, the local unit soon became a disciplined and well organised Home defence force. Certainly they looked a formidable sight as they paraded through the village behind their own Pipe Band.

Jim Mackie joined the Home Guard unofficially as a young lad in the early days of the war,

"It was mostly run by men who had served in the forces, some who even fought in the last war. It was their job to train the volunteers who were either too old or too young to join the regular forces, or else came from reserved occupations and who were not eligible to be called up.

After basic training it was the Home Guards' duty to patrol and protect the local area, the pits etc. in case of invasion, especially after the fall of France. To join the Home Guard you simply had to register at the police station and take the oath there.

The local headquarters was at the old Mission Hall, opposite Lochcraig Church, under the command of Major Hunter. Amongst the other officers that I can recall were Captain Scott and Lieutenant Taylor. Sergeant Major John 'Gunner' Hunter, an ex-Scots Guard seemed to do all the drilling of the unit, and I remember there wasn't a gun for everyone.

On training nights, the Hall was a very busy place, with drills, dismantling and re-assembly of rifles and machine guns, as well as instruction classes on everything from the use of gas masks to how to throw a hand grenade! Most weekends, we would be marched up to the rifle range, along past Parron Well, at the bottom of Benarty Hill. In addition to this we took part in route marches and the occasional church parade.

Home Guard Pipe Band

One advantage of being a member of the Home Guard was that you got a free uniform — no clothing coupons required!

An extension of the Home Guard were the Army Cadets, which were for younger boys. Lieutenant Evans was C.O. and, once again, 'Gunner' Hunter was the instructor. I joined the Cadets when it was decided that the Home Guard were to have their own Pipe Band. My uncle was to be Drum Major and he got permission from Major Hunter for me to be allowed to join the Band, on condition that I joined the Cadets. I was to do the basic training but was to be excused any further duties with them as I was a Band member.

This worked just fine for a while until Lieutenant Evans informed me that I had to continue with my Cadet duties. So, I handed in my uniform and stopped playing for the band. It didn't take long, however, before Major Hunter sent for me and told me to collect my uniform once more as his original conditions still stood. I told him that I no longer wanted any part of the Cadets, but after a while we came to a compromise — I would collect my uniform, but instead of Cadet 'flashes', I would now wear those of the Home Guard. At the tender age of thirteen, I, of course, could not officially be a member of the Home Guard, but I could be one 'unofficially'. I often wonder if I was the youngest unofficial Home Guardsman in the country!

The Pipe Band was formed in August, 1941, and its ranks included Pipe Major Alec Thomson, his two sons, Duncan and Alec, Sam Ferns, Jimmy McPherson and George Lowe. My uncle, Jim Mackie, was Drum Major, as I said, and the drummers were Jimmy Marr, Jimmy Dunn, Tommy McGurk, Barney Clarke and me.

I'll always remember the first Military funeral I attended, that of a member of the R.A.F. who came, as I recall, from Garry Park. We all wore black arm-bands and our drums were draped in black (we used Black out material). It was a very moving and sad event".

Security Measures

Anything that would hamper and slow down an invading enemy, was tried and put into operation. As already mentioned place names and street signs were removed, as were railway station signs, in order to confuse the enemy, in reality causing chaos amongst a rather bewildered populous! In the waters of the 'Meadows', large anchored floats were installed, with a strong steel cable strung between them, to prevent sea planes landing on the water. Barrage balloons were strung high above the Forth Bridge to prevent German bombers from flying low over their target and at the Naval Base up the river at Rosyth.

Precautions were taken at the Pits as well. During 1940 the Mary was joined to Glencraig by an underground line, to prevent either of the two separate companies' men being trapped underground in the event of bomb damage on the surface.

Everyone, civilian or soldier, had to carry an identity card, the National Registration card, as it was known. With the constant movement of thousands of people from one part of the country to the other, these cards were a vital part of the nation's security system. It became essential to know where anyone was at any given time, especially in the heavily populated areas which were subject to constant air attack and where the civilian casualty toll was greatest. The identity card was one method of ascertaining names of casualties and survivors. Instructions were printed clearly on the back of each card:

ALWAYS CARRY YOUR IDENTITY CARD
YOU MUST PRODUCE IT ON DEMAND BY A POLICE OFFICER IN UNIFORM OR MEMBER OF HIS MAJESTY'S ARMED FORCES IN UNIFORM ON DUTY. YOU ARE RESPONSIBLE FOR THIS CARD AND MUST NOT PART WITH IT TO ANY OTHER PERSON.
YOU MUST REPORT AT ONCE TO THE LOCAL NATIONAL REGISTRATION OFFICE IF IT IS LOST, DESTROYED, DAMAGED OR DEFACED.
IF YOU FIND A LOST IDENTITY CARD, OR HAVE IN YOUR POSSESSION A CARD NOT BELONGING TO YOURSELF OR ANYBODY IN YOUR CHARGE, YOU MUST HAND IT IN AT ONCE TO A POLICE STATION OR N.R.O. ANY BREACH OF THESE REQUIREMENTS IS AN OFFENCE PUNISHABLE BY A FINE OR IMPRISONMENT, OR BOTH.

Gas masks were issued at the beginning of the war, and had to be carried with you wherever you went. **Mrs Halliday**, then a teacher at Crosshill School, remembers the gas mask:

"After the First World War, when the troops were subjected to mustard gas attacks, which poisoned and killed thousands, the League of Nations decreed that the use of chemicals in war time was to be outlawed, under the terms of the Geneva Convention.

Despite this, the Government here took no chances, and issued everyone with a gas mask.

You had to carry it in the same way as you would carry a handbag, slung over your shoulder. Every now and then you had to try the mask, to make sure it was working properly and fitted correctly. If this wasn't the case, a Miss Agnes Page and one of her assistants would come here, usually one or two evenings a week, and she would either give you a replacement mask, or else she would repair the faulty one for you. Now that had to be done, and wherever you went you had to take the gas mask with you. You simply never went out without it, but I'm happy to say, nobody ever had to use theirs, as thankfully, we were spared any gas attacks."

Coal was still the main source of energy for all industries, as well as a domestic fuel, and to sustain the additional demands for the war effort, the Government estimated that an extra 40 million tons of coal was required, pushing output up to a staggering 270 million tons.

Steps were taken, not only to arrest the drift of manpower from the industry, but also to increase the manpower of miners by recruitment. This was achieved by introducing the 'Essential Works' order, which prevented men leaving the industry. All in all, over the 2 years, 120,000 men were released from the Armed Forces and 33,000 men transferred from other industries.

Those who were new to the industry included the Bevin Boys, young lads, some from the Public Schools, brought in to work alongside the experienced men in most of the country's pits. Glencraig and the Mary, along with other pits in the Fife coalfield, had their share of Bevin Boys, who were hostelled close to Cowdenbeath, on the road to Kelty. The lads were bussed each day to and from the Collieries.

In addition to this, the financial position of the miner was improved. A national minimum wage was introduced for the first time with guaranteed cost of living increases, as well as production and attendance bonuses. These measures greatly improved the miners lot, compared with the two decades that had gone before.

Some women were once more employed at the pits as surface workers. In 1941, the Mary Pit had at least six female workers, at the 'Picking tables', separating the redd from the coal itself. Working a 6.00 am — 2.40 pm shift, the women were paid an average of 30/- a week for the five shifts they did. Amongst those who donned the Company's blue overalls were Mrs Kate Robertson, Mrs J. Blair and Mrs Jackson, as well as Miss M. Steel and Miss C. Kerr. Two of these ladies eventually met their future husbands at the Mary Pit, Minnie Steel marrying Alex Fotheringham and Miss Kerr becoming Mrs Henderson.

During the working day, the women were allowed to use the shaftsmens' 'howff' for their tea breaks, and soon became accepted by their new workmates as equals. The women worked at the Mary for about two years or so, after which they all found jobs elsewhere, cleaner and better paid, at the likes of Rosyth and Lathalmond, luring them away from the coal mines for good.

For young lads leaving school, the prospect of a steady job in the local mines, especially if that job entailed a period of apprenticeship, was definitely something to be considered thoroughly. **James Spence** recalls,

"I started serving as an apprentice Blacksmith at Glencraig Colliery just after the war began. Most of the experienced men were in the forces at that time. Coal was vital to the war effort at that time, so Glencraig more or less worked seven days non-stop. The pit belonged to Wilson and Clyde and was independent of the other local collieries, so all the maintenance work, as far as the Blacksmiths were concerned, had to be done at the pit itself.

We made our own cages, for example. This itself was almost a full time job, as they had a lot of trouble with the shaft and the cages were constantly being damaged. The Blacksmiths were also responsible for the care and maintenance of the winding ropes and all the safety tackle pertaining to the cages. Most of the rope works had to be done either on a Sunday afternoon or evening, all the other running repairs had to be done at 'piece time' — you were never allowed to halt production at anytime.

We had other essential work, of course, such as sharpening the picks for the coal cutter and the miners' hand picks. We also had a lot of forge work, repairing some of the machinery that was unique to Glencraig Colliery. To assist us, we had a great steam engine, the likes of which you would only find in a museum nowadays. But all in all, I could safely say that Glencraig Colliery did its bit for the war effort".

The problems with the shaft at Glencraig, which Mr Spence referred to, seems to have been a constant source of trouble to the Colliery Management for a number of years. The trouble was confined to the No. 1 Shaft (the 'Big Pit Shaft'), which, it would appear, had over the years, developed a bad bend, caused by the workings of the coal seams so close to the bottom of the Pit. The slides that kept the cage steady as it travelled up and down the shaft, were fashioned from lengths of pitch pine, four or five inches thick, which were bolted into position along the length of the shaft. At the point where the bend had developed, the wooden slides took terrific punishment from the steel guides, or shoes as they were called, which were fitted on the top and bottom of the cages.

As the cages journeyed up and down the shaft, the wooden slides eventually splintered and worked themselves away from their fixings, making them at times plunge through the floor of the cage or, more often than not, catch on the cage as it made its way to the surface, shear through the two and a half inch thick roof, and jam the 'hutch' of coal. Every effort, therefore, was made to rectify the problem and minimise the loss of production caused by this fault.

On at least one occasion, in 1942, the winding drum at the 'Wee Pit' (the No. 2 shaft) snapped its cable whilst the No. 1 was, yet again, under repair. That day, all those working underground had to walk all the way to the Mary Pit before they could get home! In early 1943 the management at Glencraig tried to get around the problem by replacing all the small shoes on the cages with one large one. Unfortunately, the result was not encouraging. When a cage reached the notorious bend, it would stick firmly and would require a concentrated effort on the part of the shaftsmen before it would run freely once more. Needless to say, this experiment did not last too long!

The shaft at the Wee Pit was relatively free from such problems. For one thing the shaft remained straight. The cage was twin decked, with two hutches per deck, which meant that the pit shaft did not need to be as wide as the one at the big Pit, allowing the cages to run on a single slide at either side of it, with the guides or shoes being set in to the centre of each cage.

Rationing

Improvements at the mines were not merely confined to methods of production during the Second World War. Conditions were steadily getting better for the workers themselves.

The Mary Pit opened a canteen for its workforce in 1941. Situated between the Winding Engine House and the Lamp Cabin, the canteen provided the employees with the opportunity to buy sandwiches, soft drinks, and other snacks, before, during and after their shifts. At a time when the dreaded ration book more or less dictated what you could or could not eat, the canteen facilities no doubt went a long way in supplementing many of the works' meals. Certainly, many a young lad benefited from the occasional leftover sandwich given to him by one of the kindly canteen ladies.

For the record, the women who served in the Mary canteen during and after the war years included, Mrs Jane Anne McGill, Betty Innes, Jenny Taylor, Jen Nicholls, Minnie McCall, Mary Watson and Bessie O'Donnel.

Rationing was introduced at the start of the war, and soon not only food, but clothing, petrol and coal all went on the list of rationed goods. Clothing coupons were issued. A man's suit ('utility' of course) consisting of a jacket and a pair of trousers, could cost up to a year's supply of clothing coupons, which would mean that there was nothing left over with which to buy a shirt or a pullover, or even a pair of socks. 'Make do and mend', became a household slogan, as item after item disappeared from clothes shops everywhere.

Of course, you could always try the 'Black Market' if you could afford it. One Glencraig resident, a young man in those days, remembers going to Cowdenbeath to buy a suit . . . without coupons, but at an extortionate price! The tailor (who shall remain nameless) had premises up a narrow staircase above the shops that stood opposite the Cowdenbeath Town Clock.

"I, like many others, went there for a suit, and was measured for any style or cut that I fancied. I bought a brown double breasted type with all the trimmings. Alas, just a few weeks later I was caught in the rain, and even after, in spite of all the pressing and ironing, that suit was reduced to looking like something I'd slept in for months!"

As one by one, many types of fruit and vegetables went on the 'unobtainable' lists, another war time slogan became very popular. 'Dig for Victory' became the cry, as gardens were turned over to the growing of vegetables. Not only private gardens, but any bit of unused land was cultivated as people did what they could to produce enough food to live on. The more exotic fruits, such as bananas and even oranges, all but disappeared from the shops for the duration.

Mrs Halliday once more,

"Simply everything was rationed — all the food. Each person got one shilling and two pence worth of coupons for a week. Money was different in those days and 1/2d then was worth an awful lot more than it is today, but even then it still wasn't very much, and that's all you had to live on. Even soap was rationed".

Legend has it that there were even strict controls on the use of the Co-op's horse droppings! Before an individual could shovel these up off the street as a treat for his or her vegetable garden, they had to provide proof that they were registered with the Co-operative in the first place. Such was the institution's concern about its customer service!

A i r   R a i d   D r i l l s

Mrs Halliday also recalls the Air Raid drill at school,

"We hadn't really much alarms at all — I suppose we were really lucky. Anyway, this is what happened at school — Everybody would gather in the hall, which had a corridor off each side. Right across, closing off the entrances,

was a door, through which we made our way out to our Air Raid Shelters. Whenever the alert sounded, the children were taken out to the shelters. If they lived near at hand, any child who could be was sent off home until the 'All Clear' was sounded. All the others went into the shelters. If you think they were frightened, you couldn't be more wrong — I've seen more fuss created when a wasp came in the classroom window than was ever caused by a German air raid!

Once the raid was over, and the children who had went home came back to school we returned to normal lessons. As far as the raids were concerned, the school work was not upset much at all. Far more disruption was caused in the winter months, due to the fact that school didn't start until 10.00 a.m. then".

At this point, it is well worth consulting the school's log book for that period in 1940/41 . . .

21st October, 1940 —	The school re-opened today, after being closed for the first time for Potato Gathering. This was a war time emergency holiday of four weeks duration. Information is to hand that shelters are to be built, or better protection provided, for the pupils in case of an Air Raid.
25th October, 1940 —	Work begun on semi-sunk Air Raid shelters.
5th November, 1940—	Work has begun on two more shelters, the playground shelters being bricked up in both playgrounds.
24th January, 1941 —	Air Raid Alarm sounded at 2.30. All clear 3.20.
27th January, 1941 —	Air Raid Alarm sounded 12.25. All Clear 1.10. Keys for semi-sunk Air Raid shelters handed in, but no seating, lighting or sanitary arrangements have been installed yet.
13th February, 1941—	Air Raid Alarm at 12.07. All Clear 12.40.
19th February, 1941—	Air Raid Alarm at 10.10. All Clear 11.05 a.m.
20th February, 1941—	Air Raid Alarm at 10.55. All Clear 11.20 a.m.

Community Life

Whilst the raids continued, public meetings of all sorts were stopped in the interests of public safety. Cinemas, theatres and football grounds were all closed, and even the Scottish Football League was suspended, albeit temporarily. However, this affected people's morale to such an extent that these forms of entertainment were soon once more available to members of the public. People simply got on with their lives, in spite of the air raids, the black outs and the shortages.

Work was available, and many women, especially the younger ones, now found themselves working away from the places they had known all their lives, in factories, farms and even the forces, which all had their woman's services. The Royal Navy had their Wrens, the W.R.N.S., the army had the ATS and the R.A.F., the W.A.A.F. Then there was the Land Army, which gave women the opportunity to work on farms all over the country. All had one common aim — fill as many vacancies as possible with women, thereby releasing men for active service.

Government establishments also recruited female workers. Crombie, Rosyth and Lathalmond were a few of the most popular places, but there were many more, all offering fairly decent wages.

Even the women who could not take a job, those with young families to look after, for instance, could do their bit for the war effort. Pots and pans to build Spitfires*, gave them the opportunity of making their own small sacrifice by handing in their pans to be melted down for the aircraft industry. (Who says that recycling is a modern idea?) Iron fence posts and gates, some ornate and virtually priceless, all went into the melting pot, along with a variety of household goods, apparently to merge in another life as a Spitfire or Hurricane, although just exactly how many new aircraft were produced in this way has never been established!

Other sacrifices were made, not through choice, but rather by necessity. Amongst all the other things already in short supply was the humble cigarette! Supplies of a Turkish cigarette — 'Pashas' — were never in any danger of running out, however. According to those who remember them, 'Pashas' were the last resort for a smoker! Only an addict of the weed would touch them. They tasted vile, but the taste was nothing in comparison to the nasty smell they gave off. If smoked in a confined space, the humble 'Pasha' could completely ruin a whole theatre or cinema audience's evening, according to 'Pasha' folklore!

During the years of the war, a great many morale-boosting campaigns were run, such as 'Salute the Army' week or 'Salute the Navy' and 'theme dances' were held, such as 'Help Buy A Spitfire' dances. Jumble sales and whist drives were held. The Fire Services at Crosshill opened their premises to the public in an effort to raise money and held a variety of events during the open day. There was great public demand for all sorts of events like these and all helped keep morale high, during the darkest days of the war.

By 1943, a Prisoner of War camp had been set up at Capledrae. At first, the camp held mostly Italian prisoners who were given more or less the

Footnote: * A Combat Aircraft.

freedom to roam the area as they pleased. Later on, increasing numbers of German prisoners were sent here, and they were restricted far more in their movements than the Italians had ever been. The majority were put to work on farms throughout the district, and remained there long after the eventual end of the war. The last of these men were repatriated in 1948.

V.E. Day, when it came at long last, brought scenes of joy all over the country. **James Spence**, for the purpose of this book, wrote of his recollections of that day,

"V.E. Day was celebrated in my area by a Piper going round the streets, summoning people to come to the front of the manse, which was floodlit, to sing and dance. There was a great bonfire lit and a lot of folk took this opportunity to burn their black out material. Fireworks were available from the local newsagent's shop; they must have been stored away during the war. I remember that quite a few fireworks were exploded in the local cinema that memorable night!

We had six years of rationing and black outs and sometimes depressing news, but we came through it. When you see what other people endured, you can say that, on the whole, we were very lucky in this area".

The Second World War finally over, the mining industry which had been under Government control, was set for Nationalisation as the newly elected Labour Government came to power. The miners looked forward to this with relief and pleasure for surely a new day was dawning with better prospects for those who had suffered so much in the past.

· CHAPTER 8 ·
The People's Pits

In the post war Britain of the late 1940s and 1950s, great things were expected. The country, tired but victorious after six long years of war, went to the polls and sent a Labour Government into power with a landslide victory. The Government of Clement Attlee promised sweeping changes, including a free National Health Service for every citizen and the Nationalisation of many industries, coal mining being one of them.

The Nationalisation of the Mining Industry came into being on New Year's Day, 1947. From May 5th, of that year, working hours below ground were reduced and the working week fell from 44 hours, on average, to 37½ for all face workers. Wages would rise for all mine workers and annual holidays would now be paid, instead of the idle time of the past.

Some of the changes brought by nationalisation were not, at first, apparent, however. **James Spence** recalls the government take over, from a Glencraig worker's point of view,

". . . apart from the flags with the letters N.C.B. on them, and a board at the colliery entrance which proudly announced 'THIS COLLIERY IS MANAGED BY THE PEOPLE FOR THE PEOPLE' (indeed, the cynical comment of the time, amongst miners was 'It's the same team in different jerseys!'), there was little noticeable changes during the takeover period. Glencraig, however, now gained the services of the Central Workshops at Cowdenbeath.

One important development not long after Nationalisation was the introduction of the five-day working week, although due to the great demand for coal, this was never fully implemented. Most men continued to work an eleven day fortnight until the mid '50s at least. For the tradesmen at the Pit, the situation was more or less the same. We worked seven days a week, only now we were being paid time-and-a-half for Saturday work, and double time on a Sunday".

There did seem to be a general optimism, as far as the future of the coal-mining industry was concerned, however. Two years before nationalisation, when Glencraig was celebrating its jubilee, W.H. Telfer told the assembled guests that, as far as the future was concerned, the Fife coalfields had at least 200 years worth of coal reserves, more than any other field in the country. Glencraig, he stated, in particular, had almost a hundred years of reserves and he was convinced that, come the 1960s, Fife would be the leading field for production of coal, in the whole of the country.

Mr Telfer could not have been more wrong!

The facts were that when the industry was nationalised, the new National Coal Board 'inherited' a ramshackle industry, run down for years by its former owners, who had consistently failed to invest in new machinery, preferring to take the coal that was easiest to get at and abandoning perfectly good workings in order to cut costs. Some of the members of the Benarty Mining Heritage Group can recall the management at Glencraig and Mary pits hastily repainting old and virtually useless machinery in an effort to impress the Government Inspectors who came to set price figures to cover the Nationalisation scheme and compensate the Mine owners. A considerable amount of worthless equipment gained a good price for the owners, all because of a coat of paint!

It may be a fair commentary on the former coal owners penny-pinching attitude to look at how things were at Glencraig when Davie Dickson started there as an apprentice in 1937. At the time Davie was considered lucky to get an apprenticeship when most boys could only hope for a job on the picking tables, or else as a 'bogey laddie' down the 'Wee' Pit.

At the Pit, Andrew Crowe was the agent, Willie Black was the manager, and the Chief Engineer was 'Big Jack' Paragreen. **Davy** started in the stores under Willie Justice and he recalls,

"One of my first jobs in the store was to collect all the nuts and bolts which had been used or discarded by the men who had worked on the weekend maintenance shifts. These bits had to be brought back to the store and re-threaded for future use — nothing was wasted at Glencraig in those days".

He then goes on to say how, after his first year, he worked in the Engineer's shop, under Johnny Fosyth, to learn his trade,

"When I look back now, it never ceases to amaze me, when I think of all that was produced in the 'shop' — Nothing was bought from outside if it could possibly be made at the Colliery — most of the gear for the cages, including all the suspension chains, haulages and coal-cutting picks (as well as the occasional girdle and poker!)"

Whilst this may all have been good training, it certainly couldn't have been cost-effective, and it indicates how reluctant the company were to spend any money at all.

On the other hand it is only fair to say that when Davie went to the Mary, which was controlled by the Fife Coal Company he found a completely different attitude. Whatever else they may have been as employers in the mid-war years, they were a progressive company in terms of training their people and in their mining engineering techniques, and deserve credit for that.

Modernisation

Certainly under nationalisation, investment was made in the Industry producing radical changes, both underground and on the surface.

At Glencraig in the mid-fifties the most notable improvement came with the change over from the steam winder to a more modern, electrical one. This meant that the men who had previously been working in the fireholes had to be deployed elsewhere in the colliery.

A new Pithead was constructed and machinery installed to cope with the installation and running of the modern Mine Cars, which replaced the hutches as the main mode of transport for coal and debris underground. Only the Big Pit was reconstructed to make room for the cars, the Wee Pit continuing to use the hutches. In the Big Pit, the mine cars were to be pulled by locomotive engines, replacing the old method of over rope and under rope haulage, which had been the practice for years.

Improvements were not confined to Glencraig Colliery. On the 8th November, 1952, the new pithead baths at the Mary Colliery were opened at an official ceremony. At a total cost to the Coal Board of some £49,578, the baths had facilities which included almost 800 pairs of lockers for the Mary's employees as well as the fifty new showers to be used by miners and Pit officials. This was part of the general improvement plans put into operation at coal mines all over Scotland. As the brochure produced at the opening stated:

'With the opening of Mary Colliery Pithead baths installation, there will be 102 baths installations in operation at board undertakings in the Scottish division, providing bathing facilities for 65,138 workmen'.

A cycle store, which could easily accommodate up to twenty bicycles and two motorcycles opened at the same time as the pithead baths, and plans were already well underway to provide the Colliery with a fully equipped, purpose-built Medical Centre, as well as an extension to the existing Canteen which had opened in 1941.

The opening day's programme of events ran as follows:-

Chairman's Remarks	—	Mr Alex Clark, Colliery Manager.
Official Opening Remarks	—	Mr John Jennings, Repairer at Mary Colliery.
Inspection of Baths		
Adjourn for Tea		
Presentation	—	To Mr John Jennings by Mr George Mullin, Area General Manager.
Remarks	—	Mr P. Ness, District Secretary, National Union of Mineworkers, Fife, Clackmannan and Kinross District.
Vote of Thanks	—	Councillor James Robertson, Delegate, N.U.M., Mary Colliery.

The brochure carried this tribute to the aforementioned John Jennings,

"Mr Jennings is employed as a repairer at Mary Colliery and resides at 26 Mannering Street, Lochore. He was born in Cumberland, the eldest son in a family of seven. He started work in the Mining industry at 12 years of age and worked in the Cumberland and Northumberland Coalfields. When he started work he was paid 1/3d. per day but at 15 years of age he was given a man's job and received a man's wage of 4./3d. per day.

Mr Jennings came to Mary Colliery in 1917; his hobby is gardening and he is a pipe smoker. He has been employed in the coal industry for 63 years (!) except for a period of six months when he joined the Police Force but left due to the small wage being paid of 21/- per week. It is a rather signficant feature that Mr Jennings will be 76 years of age on Christmas day, 1952".

The statutory retirement at 65 had obviously not come into being in John Jennings day!

In fact, up until January 1st of that year, there was no State Pension Scheme to speak of, so it was not unusual for men of Mr Jennings age to be working in the industry, above and below ground. It was not until the middle of the 1950s that the age of retirement was set at 65.

Future Leaders

While one man was coming to the end of a lifetime's service in the coal mines, another was just starting out in the industry.

Willie Clarke, a present day local Councillor, was then just a boy, beginning his working career at the local pit.

"I started work in Glencraig Colliery in 1950, on the Table, where the coal was screened. The hours at that time were 12.36 to 9.00 p.m. on the back-shift and 6.00 a.m. to 2.24 p.m. on days, for which the pay was 7/4½d. — approximately 37p in today's money — per shift. A year later, when I reached the age of 16 and began working underground, I got 11/8d. for my shift of 7½ hours plus 'Winding time'.*

"When I started work, we had only one week's annual holiday. Christmas day was just another working day; this was the situation until 1953, when we finally got a fortnight's annual break. Glencraig certainly had its fair share of disputes during the fifties, when relationships between the management and the men tended to be very poor. The N.U.M. committee produced a monthly magazine at that time, called 'Pit Bits', which presumably had taken over from the old 'Crow Picker'.

Over the years, the Glencraig N.U.M. Branch was at the forefront of struggles, both locally and nationally, and indeed produced three Scottish executive members; Lawrence Daly, who later became the National Secretary, the late Johny Stewart and myself. I think this must stand as some kind of a record in Scotland".

Lawrence Daly, whom Willie refers to, had started work at Glencraig in 1939 and by 1947 had risen to the rank of Secretary of the Glencraig N.U.M. Lawrence's father, James had been an active trade-unionist and had been victimised for his political beliefs in the aftermath of the '26 strike. The Daly family were forced to leave their 'tied' house, as James sought work in other coalfields. Around 1937 or 1938, the family returned to Fife, where James had been promised work at Glencraig. Eventually, in 1939, Lawrence followed his father down the Pit, beginning work as a hewer.

After the war, Lawrence, by this time a member of the World Youth Council, was invited to visit the Soviet Union along with other members of the Youth Council — James Callaghan, the future Labour Prime Minister, and the actor, Gordon Jackson. Daly later wrote about his experiences there, in his book 'A Young Miner Sees Russia'. The publication of which brought him to the attention of miners in other parts of the country.

Footnote: * Wage Rates for Youths in 1949.

Surface		Underground	
14 years 7/½ d	(35p)	15 years 9/5d	(47p)
15 years 7/4d	(37p)	16 years 10/4¼	(52p)
16 years 8/3d	(41p)	17 years 12/1¼	(61p)
17 years 9/2d	(46p)	18 years 15/1¼	(75p)
18 years 12/-	(60p)	19 years 15/2¾	(76p)
19 years 12/3½	(61p)	20 years 15/4¼	(77p)
20 years 12/7½	(63p)		

He also wrote other material, which did not exactly endear him to the management, *". . . I started a local typescript monthly called 'Pit Bits', really an anti-management sheet. I was very active in the Communist Party, but left after Kruschev denounced the crimes of Stalin. With a few local friends, Charlie Boyle, John Cormack, George McDonald and John Keenan of Dundonald, I founded the Fife Socialist League and published its monthly newsheet, 'The Socialist'.*

Shortly afterwards, I became a County Councillor for Ballingry and was encouraged to stand for Parliament. My supporters, during that campaign of 1959, worked like Trojans, and we got good support, although the Labour Party's huge majority meant that I lost my deposit".

Lawrence spent his working life, actively fighting for his fellow N.U.M. comrades, becoming National Secretary in 1968, defeating the future President of the N.U.M., Joe Gormley. The two men remained close friends and were instrumental in winning the national strike against the N.C.B. in 1972 and the Heath Government in 1974. In 1984, Lawrence was advised by his doctors to retire due to his generally poor health, and although he no longer takes an active part in the Trade Union movement, his name is recalled with fondness by miners everywhere.

N.U.M. Summer School

Goodbye Glencraig

As Glencraig Pit was renovated with the onset of Nationalisation, Glencraig Village was also to change completely during the same period. Fife County Council had long been aware of the poor housing conditions and generally unhealthy environment in which the villagers lived.

For years the great 'bings', or spoil heaps, which dominated the skyline and polluted the atmosphere, had been a constant source of ill health amongst the inhabitants. Dust and dirt from the bings got everywhere, depending on which way the wind was blowing.

In the late 1930s, when internal combustion had these tips well alight, the strong sulphurous fumes were noticeable for miles around. As one resident remembers, *"even the pillow you laid your head on at night reeked of sulphur"*.

In 1927, the colliery began to tip the spoil and redd by the Avenue, so that it was eventually completely blocked off to pedestrians and vehicles alike. An alternative road was made detouring around the bottom of the twin peaked bing, heading up to Glencraig House. Add to all this, the growing problems caused by subsidence and it is not hard to see why the council decided at long last, to act.

Glencraig Rows and Group

Plans were laid to rehouse the inhabitants in a healthier atmosphere, at Ballingry. The new housing arrangements, which would create the township of Ballingry, included the rehousing of practically all the residents of Glencraig. Ballingry was to get housing for upwards of 8,000 people.

Month after month, people were being resettled in their new homes as row by row, the old Miners' cottages disappeared forever. The modern community of Ballingry had its beginnings in those Post-War days of 1947 onwards. Fife County Council's ambitious plans were outlined in an article which first appeared in the 1950s.

"For the Ballingry—Lochore area the main object... is to provide for the re-location of part of the community further north on safer ground and among more attractive surroundings. 'The plan envisages the ultimate clearance of North and South Glencraig'.

Waverley Street

Waverley Street Group

Allocated for new housing areas are:- About six acres on the north side of Benarty Road: about four acres on the south site between Ballingry and Lochore: about an acre in Loanhead Avenue: about half an acre north-east of Ballingry: about three acres south-west of the Institute at Lochore: and about one and half acres north of Crosshill".

The Council also planned a 'green-belt' surrounding the new houses. On this would be situated a new football pitch, close to Loanhead Avenue, and a playing field at Ballingry High School. New schools were to be built, in addition to those already there, and a nursery school was planned for the centre of Ballingry.

At about the same time, the village of Lochore too saw many changes. A number of its original streets were rerouted to cope with the increase in domestic traffic, and the majority of the old Miners' cottages were pulled down to make way for more modern housing. A few of the old cottages did remain, although the majority of these were modernised and thus the face of the village changed forever.

Over the early 50's the exodus from Glencraig continued, and finally, by 1962, owing to insufficient number of pupils, Glencraig school was closed. So the village of Glencraig all but disappeared, leaving only the Miners' Institute as a landmark, and, more importantly, as a meeting place for many of the villages' former residents in the years to come.

Village reunions take place there from time to time, and it may be, as a result of the interest generated by the knowledge that this book was being produced, that such a reunion was advertised in the Central Fife Times, to be held on October 23rd, 1992.

This would seem to suggest that, no matter its past history, the village of Glencraig engendered a nostalgic appeal for those who once lived there, missing perhaps, the special sense of community which typifies mining villages and which is now, sadly, almost lost.

Hopes Dashed

Despite the early optimism of the miners that they could look forward to a period of stability and prosperity in a Nationalised Industry, they were to be bitterly disappointed.

Certainly, Nationalisation had meant massive investment, and indeed, major new sinkings, such as that of the Rothes Colliery.

However, a number of factors were operating against the miners' interests.

The Rothes, for example, proved to be a 'white elephant' — a fact that many of the older miners had predicted, alleging that the sinking had been a deliberate ploy on the part of the former Coal companies in anticipation of massive compensation.

The Coal industry was indeed over-burdened with heavy compensation payments for pits which had been worked only with concern for an immediate profit in the past, had lacked investment, and were now costly to operate.

Added to this was the unrestrained import of temporarily cheap oil from the Middle East, which successive governments had failed to control, ignoring the predictions that the country would pay a high price for this in the long term, which, indeed, it did.

The consequence of all these factors was that many collieries began to be looked on, in accountants' terms, as inefficient, and towards the end of the 1950s and into the early 1960s, there was a massive programme of closures within the industry, with dozens of pits going from West Fife alone.

The process began with the closure of the 'Dora' and 'Jenny Gray' pits, at Cowdenbeath and Lochgelly and the Benarty mine in 1958. For a while it seemed as if Glencraig and the Mary would manage to 'ride out' the slump and continue to be the major source of employment for the district. Unfortunately, this was not to be.

The first blow fell in May 1966 when it was announced that Glencraig Colliery, after a lifetime of coal production was to close. R. W. Parker, the Scottish Division Chairman of the National Coal Board sealed Glencraig's fate when he announced that production would cease there on July 16th, the beginning of the Fife 'trades fortnight'.

It was claimed that Glencraig had been losing money for several years. Indeed, since the Nationalisation of the coal Industry in 1947, it was said that the Coal Board had lost some £5,000,000 at the colliery, with the position worsening as the years went by, until the Colliery was now losing £1 for every ton of coal produced.

The closure was reluctantly agreed to by the unions involved at Glencraig and Mr Parker had given an assurance that almost all the employees would be redeployed at other pits throughout the country, and elsewhere. Seafield Colliery, in particular, was developing rapidly at that time and it was confidently assumed that it would shortly have a workforce of some 3,000.

Most of the younger Glencraig men would, no doubt, find alternative employment there.

Dr Jeremy Bray, Parliamentary Secretary to the Minister of Power, who had been on a two day visit to the Fife Coalfield when the closure plans had been revealed, said at the time,

". . . the Ministry wanted to make sure the miner knew he was working in an industry where his prospects were as good as anywhere else.

. . . the miner should have the same choice of jobs as any other worker. The Ministry could not afford the present drain in manpower out of the industry nor could it afford to keep men less productively employed in obsolete pits". Despite the closure of Glencraig Colliery, Dr Bray was *". . . confident that the mining industry in Fife had an essential role to play in a diversified industrial economy".*

In the event this proved to be about as true as Telfer's statement in 1945 about the '100 years of workable resources'.

However the closure of Glencraig, with the loss of 650 jobs, brought immediate problems for some of the other pits in the district and would cast serious doubts over the future of the Mary, as well as the pits at Kinglassie, Lumphinnans and the Minto Colliery, all major employers in the area.

One of the working seams at the Mary had to be sealed off in the month that the Glencraig closure was announced, due to an underground fire which had made it unworkable. Notices had been posted at the Mary asking for the names of any men who would be willing to transfer to other pits. It seemed that the Mary was preparing itself for the worst. This proved to be the case.

Farewell — Mary

The Mary too was to follow its older neighbour into the history books and both pits ceased production on the same day — the Friday before 'the Fair holidays'.

For over sixty years, the Mary Colliery had given work to almost every family in Lochore in one way or another. Not only those families of men who worked in the pit but also those who had set up small businesses in the district — the shopkeepers and tradesmen etc., all depended on the prosperity of the Mary Pit for their income.

Now no longer would the men walk the short distance from their homes to the colliery at the start of each new working day. Instead, buses would leave the village for the Michael, Seafield and other pits further afield. The mines at Bogside and Solsgirth would now provide the wages that the local pits could not. Benarty was no longer a coal producer of any importance.

One of the last men employed at the Mary Colliery was Arthur McGachie, who was still there long after production had ceased*. **Arthur** remembers the last few weeks in the life of the once great Pit clearly,

"All work underground ended on the 24th September, 1966†. Only a small amount of the machinery was ever returned to the surface when the pit closed. Officials from some of the other collieries came and took what they wanted and arranged transport to haul it away. The cages and winding ropes were run off in the end. Three steam 'locos' were left there, along with about a hundred wagons and several miles of railsidings.

We were instructed to get rid of all the books and paperwork from the office, along with all the office furniture, the desks and tables, chairs etc. So, after getting written permission from Mr Peter Sinclair, who was in charge of the demolition work, we piled everything into one big heap and set it alight. The fire burned for over twenty four hours.

In January of the next year, they started moving the remaining wagons. They were shunted into a long line and a steam loco came and pulled them away, fifty empty wagons at a time. It took two days before the sidings were finally emptied.

The next job was to get rid of the great bings, which by this time had been on fire for more than a year. The dust and smoke were everywhere and the fumes were awful. Anyway, the redd bing was only about fifty yards or so from the No. 2 Pit shaft, where the water had risen to about 300 yards up the shaft itself, so it was decided to fill this in using the debris from the bing. They filled up several tipper trucks with the redd and dumped the whole lot down the shaft. Finally, a scrap company came and started to demolish what was left of the pithead. There was still quite a bit of work left for us to do, as the ground was covered in rubbish — bits of wood and coal debris — which had to be moved away. This didn't take too long though, and I and my two workmates, Archie Davidson and John McDonald, were informed that our services would not be required after February 16th, 1968.

On that day, I was dayshift and due to finish up at 2.00 p.m. Jock and Archie came over at about 1.00, Jock bringing a bottle of whisky along with him.

Footnotes: * The last manager at the Mary Pit was Malcolm McGugan, who held the position for fourteen years. McGugan also became Chairman of the Lochore Miners' Welfare Institute, as well as Chairman of the Lochore House Youth Club..
† All work underground also ended at Glencraig Colliery on the same day.

As it neared 2.00, Jock was ready for binging!"

So, at long last, we took one lingering look at where the pits used to be, said our goodbyes to the Mary, and walked away. There were no tears, no gloom, only memories. Sadly, Jock and Archie are no longer with us, but they will be remembered".

Thus, after three score years and ten, ended the life of the collieries which had in turn dominated the lives of the people in the Benarty area. Now, only the bings remained, silent monuments to the past.

The Meadows and Mary Pit Structure

The Meadows

In time, these bings themselves would be removed in what was described as "Britain's biggest landscape facelift". The reclamation of the land from Lochore all the way to Kelty, began the year after the Mary and Glencraig closed down.

The first phase of the £1 million pound scheme at the Meadows was underway by November, 1967, and had already attracted the attention of several industrialists and businesses, nationwide. **The Dunfermline Press** reported,

"A five-year facelift project by the County Planning Committee will transform four square miles of the most derelict land in Fife — the Industrial Revolution's squalid legacy of pit bings, bogs and mineral subsidence lochs — into a lovely landscape with a lido, recreation grounds, rich farming land and attractive industrial sites.

. . . with the completion of the plan, the area would be turned into a beauty spot, with sailing and water ski-ing, swimming, fishing and golfing among its attractions. Farming would benefit too, by regaining 1,035 acres that a century ago, were pastures green".

The plans were certainly ambitious.

Approximately 10 million tons of pit waste were moved from the old pit-bings and used to recontour the surrounding area. The Mary Loch would be converted into a huge recreation centre ideal for watersports, once its area was reduced from 260 to 130 acres. Picnic grounds, with camping and caravan sites close by, transformed the complex into a major tourist attraction, creating work in an area, already suffering the effects of the loss of its coal mining days.

The project involved the co-operation of the National Coal Board, local landowners, and farmers, as well as the local and County Councils. This, however was not always forthcoming. In May 1969, for instance, a plan to remove the slurry from Glencraig to nearby Bowhill as part of the land reclamation project, had to be shelved, after objections that it would cause a major dust nuisance at Bowhill.

Hold ups and objections not withstanding, the County Council's 'pipe dream' eventually became reality in March, 1975, with the official opening of the £1 million Lochore Meadows Recreational Park.

And behind the first green of the trim Golf Course, stands the old Mary No. 2 Pithead Frame, a constant reminder of by-gone days.

· CHAPTER 9 ·

Role Of The Institutes

Throughout the life of the villages that formed the communities of Benarty, the one constant factor for many people had to be the Miners Institute. In many ways, the institutes were the forerunners of modern community centres providing for the needs of a great many people in various ways. In short, the Institute was the hub of village life.

In the beginning, the Institutes were virtually 'male only' establishments, used for everything from Public Meetings to Boxing bouts. As one of the few places in the neighbourhood to boast a radio set, the Institute very often found itself filled to capacity, especially on the days of an International football match, when hordes of local men would gather to listen to the commentary from Hampden Park, and beyond!

And the Institutes had their characters amongst the men who frequented them. Take, for instance, the McCormack brothers, Ned, Joe and Charlie (whose sons, incidentally, joined the call for volunteers to the International Brigades and went to Spain in the late 1930's) — these three old 'Worthies' from Glencraig took their game of dominoes seriously. Many a day, the concentration of other players would be shattered, as Charlie completely oblivious to all others in the games room, would roar loudly and passionately at either Ned or Joe, for some indiscretion, real or imagined, that he felt they had committed, when playing a particular domino!

And characters such as these are still recalled with affection in the Institutes of today.

Glencraig Institute

In January 1904, the trustees of the East of Scotland Public House Trust completed the purchase of three and a half acres of ground at Glencraig from a local JP, Mr J. Nelson. The trustees intention was to build a large hall, complete with a library and recreation room on part of the land, using the remaining ground as a Public Park. They also proposed, in the future, to form a local 'Gothenburgh Society'.

Less than eighteen months later, in July 1905, the first part of these plans was realised with the opening of the building, by Sir Ralph Anstruther, who, in his opening speech, informed his audience that, not only was he a member

Glencraig Miners Institute

of the Trust, but he was also a member of the Temperance Society, and he firmly believed that the profits made from the sale of alcohol and other refreshments should go towards further beneficial causes within the community.

In the following year, the Public House Trust, in their annual report, stated that the Glencraig 'experiment' had been the first they had attempted in an effort to divert the Miners away from the habit of heavy drinking. Profits from the venture had been used to complete part of the Institute at Glencraig, which comprised of a Billiard Room, with two tables, a Reading Room and a Recreation Room. The total cost, so far, had been almost £900, which the Trust considered well spent, because of the beneficial effects it was having on the miners themselves.

The report stated with pride, *"The miner can now have a little refreshment at the 'Goth' then return with his friends, to pass the evening in the Institute, instead of spending the whole evening, as before, over drinking..."*

By 1909 it was reported in the local press that the Trust now intended to build a hall and a Caretakers house, which would cost somewhere in the region of £900.

The Glencraig Institute's annual General Meeting was held that same year, on 16th of December, with Mr Park, of the School House, presiding. The principal matter discussed was the *'inability of the Public House Trust to live up to their earlier promises to spend more on the Institute'.*

This was, it was felt 'a severe drag to social progress'. The committee estimated that the Trust had made approximately £2,000 profit annually from the 'Goth', yet only a pauper's allowance had been given back for the benefit of the local people over the last three years.

It was no good making profits if the Trust merely intended holding onto them, therefore the committee demanded *". . . the Trust carry out their promised extensions to the Institute"*.

The first A.G.M. held after the end of the Great War took place on the 21st of December, 1918. Charlie Barclay, as Chairman of the meeting, was able to announce to the members that the committee, which had taken over the running of the Institute from the Public House Trust some nine months previously, were now showing a profit of £22.2s.1½., of which, £20 had already been lodged with the bank. The following members were then elected to the committee — J. Martin, C. Ward, W. Aird, D. Munro and J. R. Salmond.

Finally, the Chairman thanked Mr W. H. Telfer, General Manager of the Wilson and Clyde Coal Company, for the silver cup and gold medal presented by the Company for the Institute's annual Billiards competition.

Now completely in the hands of his members, Glencraig Institute went from strength to strength. A loan from the Coal Company in 1920 went towards the installation of 'cinematograph' equipment in the big hall, whilst a supply of electricty to the building came directly from the colliery itself. The members themselves built a boundary fence around the premises and also renewed the road between the Institute and the 'Goth'.

Workers at the colliery had agreed to a 1d. deduction from their wages per week, to pay for the upkeep of the Institute. A £55 grant from the Coal Company allowed the committee to buy new books for the library, whilst the committe now had sufficient funds to purchase the ground immediately in front of the building, and a new road could now be built from the entrance to the main hall. The Institute acquired a further two billiard tables, and, by January 1st, 1921, the Picture House in the Institute's big hall — grandly known as 'The Glencraig People's Picture Palace' — was opened by Mr J. Heath of Edinburgh, being appointed as the first 'Picture Palace' manager.

What of events held in the Institute? **James Rowan** recalls,

"The large hall, like any other Miners' Institute, was used for all kinds of functions, such as weddings, concerts, dances and public meetings. Many

famous people spoke there through the years — Tom Mann, Harry Pollitt, Willie Gallacher, Arthur Horner, Abe and Alex Moffat, Lawrence Daly and Arthur Scargill.

I remember in 1932, a notice in the Institute, stating that a certain company would be demonstrating a new invention, to most of us — a microphone! The demonstration would be in the big hall, on a given night, and, as admission was free, predictably, on the night in question, the hall was full. Many of the audience took this opportunity to try singing into this new 'contraption'. Among those I remember singing that night were Jimmy, Joe and Willie (Jude) Russell, Jock 'Tinney' McGuire and Pete Ward, who, in later years, ran a 'second-hand' shop at what is now the entrance to the Meadows Park. Pete, I remember had a surprisingly nice voice.

Mention of 'Tinney' McGuire takes me back to earlier that same year. I had just left school, and had started working.

It was a Saturday night, and I, along with two pals, was wandering through the streets and rows in Lochgelly, when we heard dance music coming from the wooden building known locally as the 'Band Hut', so we decided to 'keek' in. The floor was a seething mass of dancers, whilst on the small stage, was 'Tinney', with an enormous megaphone, which he was desperately trying to hold up to his mouth, whilst he sang his heart out! The song he sang, I remember, was a famous 'western' ballad of that time — 'Wagon Wheels' ''.

Throughout the next two decades, Glencraig Institute continued to play its part as a centre for village social life, with Public meetings, concerts, dances and weddings taking place there. Major public events were also held in the Institutes hall.

In early 1945, for example, whilst the War was coming to its conclusion, Glencraig Institute played host to a dinner celebrating a milestone in the life of the village colliery. On Monday, 12th March, the official dinner was held to mark the 50th anniversary of the cutting of the first sod at the Glencraig Colliery in 1895.

Amongst those present that day, were a large number of retired miners and their wives, as well as some of Glencraig's longest serving employees. John Duncan, the colliery's Cashier was chairman of the proceedings and the guests of honour were none other than Mr and Mrs Telfer, returning to the village for the first time in several years.

By the end of the Second World War, the Institute at Glencraig was still the hub of village life for many people. The weekly deduction from the

Glencraig Colliery's employees' wage packets, no more than a few pence, ensured that the Institute had sufficient funds with which to supply its membership with a number of varied facilities.

The Billiards Room was very popular and the Institute fielded teams who played in the local Billiards Leagues. It had a Reading Room where the daily newspapers were all available to anyone who wanted to read them and it also provided a library service in the days before the Council built Glencraig's own Public Library.

The Hall was in great demand for dances, socials and 'Whist Drives' that were very popular then, as well as for the political meetings and debates that took place there. When the likes of William Gallacher or Willie Hamilton came to talk at the Institute in those post-war days, they were always sure of a 'packed house' at Glencraig. Bob Harrower, a local Labour Pary member (as well as an expert on Robert Burns) challenged Lawrence Daly, then a young member of the Communist Party, to a debate in the Institute, and again the Hall was filled.

Outside, in the Institute grounds were the Bowling Green and gardens which proved an attractive feature of the village, especially in the summer months.

At least three people deserve a mention for the work they put in to the general upkeep of Glencraig Institute in that period just after the War. Johnny Martin, who lived in the Institute's house and maintained the place along with Jack Findlay who assisted in the running of the Bowling green and upkeep of the large gardens. Inside the building itself, Miss Helen O'Neil (Mrs Carr) ran the small office, controlling the use of the billiards and snooker tables, as well as selling soft drinks and snacks etc.

In May 1955, the Billiard tables were removed as that part of the Institute was turned into a bar, when a Liquor Licence was eventually granted for the premises.

Although Glencraig village itself all but disappeared in the mid-1950s, and its colliery closed less than ten years later, the Institute still maintained its position in local circles as a centre for 'Village folk', who came regularly from their new homes in Ballingry, to once more enjoy the various dances, concerts, bingo and other attractions that the Institute provided.

Changes in social behaviour, however, and the failure to attract young members of the community, saw the decline, which affected a great many clubs in the 1980s, have its effects on Glencraig Institute also, especially as fewer and fewer people living in Ballingry had any personal association with the old village.

Today, a hard working committee struggles valiantly simply to make ends meet and the officials are: Chairman — Michael Keicher; Vice-chairman — Johnston Blake; Secretary — Tom McMaihin; Treasurer — Willie Clarke: Committe Members — John Alexander, John Davie, Kay Bennie*, Sandy Waugh, Joe Waugh, John Nardone, Sammy Little, Jackie Wright.

It would be a tragedy, indeed, if this particular link with the former village was ever severed, and the Institute was to close. For is it not true that its very existence is a constant reminder of Glencraig's mining past?

Lochore Institute

Built on its present site in 1934, and fitting snugly into the junction of Abbotsford Road and Main Street, the Lochore Miners' Institute creates an impressive and pleasant picture.

The Institute's imposing structure and clean exterior gives no indication that here stands this village's last remaining link with its mining past. Further along Main Street parallel to the building's frontage, towards the 'village' hall and in through the impressive iron gates is another example of the Institute's commitment to the community. Close to the main building is the relatively new Bowling Pavilion, and on its right the retired men's shelter.

There is no clue that under the trim and tidy Bowling Green before you, the very origins of the village lie buried, For here, in by-gone days stood the Miners' Rows — Caravan Row, Cannongate and Candlemakers Row, picturesque in name, considerably less so in reality.

In the attempt to trace the origins of the Lochore Miners Institute, we are particulary grateful for the kind help given by Mr James Campbell, of Mucklestane Cottage, who provided much invaluable information.

It seems that in late 1909, a small committee, formed by the Miners of Lochore, approached the Managing Director of the Fife Coal Company, Charles A. Carlow, asking him to help in providing a Reading Room in the area. Carlow gifted a double house to the committee, complete with free rent and coal. The house was situated on 'New Road', which would later become known as Abbotsford Road.

So it was, that on the 22nd February, 1910, Lochore's first Reading Room was officially opened by Mr Carlow. The F.C.C. also gifted furnishings for the building, and its Chairman presented the miners with a new billiard table.

Footnote: * Uniquely, a woman on a Miners Club Committee!

Lochore Miners Institute

Lochore Colliery Brass Band at the old Institute and Reading Room

The building soon proved popular in Lochore. So much so, that by 1912, the committee decided that the existing premises were far too small to cater for the village's needs, and a large extension was called for. This extension would provide, amongst other things, a fully equipped billiard room, with four tables, a 'recreation' room with various games and a greatly enlarged library.

These ambitious plans were eventually realised by a generous loan from the Coal Company. On the 10th of May, 1913, the extensive renovation work was completed and once more, an opening ceremony was held. Mrs Mary Carlow, after whom the local pit had been named, officially opened a new public park that day, the ground having been donated by the directors of the Fife Coal Company. Mrs Carlow was presented with a gold padlock, and her husband, who had presided over the event, was given a gold key. Among the assembled guests was Mr Roden, manager of the Mary Pit and, the then president, of the Reading Room committee. The Bowhill Brass Band was in attendance, to play to the gathering and, by all accounts, a splendid time was had by one and all, before the distinguished guests were treated to a 'Cake and Wine' banquet in the 'Red Goth' hall.

On the 18th of November, 1931, the Miners' Welfare Committee for this area set aside the sum of £10,000 for the building of a new Institute in the Lochore area. Amongst several possible sites mooted were Masonic ground at Crosshill, Tushielaw, and the site of the tramway terminus, known locally as the 'burned building' (the site of the present day chemists and surgery).

Tushielaw Cottage

One week later, a deputation from the Welfare Committee visited the area and decided that the site for the new Institute must be in Lochore itself, effectively ruling out the Masonic site and also allaying the fears of both Lochore and Glencraig committees that a central institute would be forced upon them — an idea that neither side wished to contemplate, the rivalry between the two villages being, to say the least, intense.

On the 15th of September, 1934, the new Institute was completed on the Tushielaw site, at a cost of £13,200. Mr G. Hutchison, the then manager of the Mary Pit, presided over events, whilst the opening ceremony itself was carried out by **Mr W. Adamson**, Secretary of the Fife Miners' Union, who in his opening address said,

"A new Bowling Green would also have been provided, but the Government cut the Welfare Grant from 1d per ton to ½d. I am hopeful the levy will be restored, sooner, rather than later, so that the Welfare can continue, to provide facilities for mining communities".

Dr Sinclair accepted the new Institute on behalf of the local committee, and afterwards, in a short speech to the assembly, Charles Reid, the Managing Director of the Fife Coal Company, admitted that he had often differed with the committee, as he had always been in favour of one central building, serving both Lochore and Glencraig. At one particularly heated meeting he had been told, quite bluntly, that *". . . there could be no dealings between the 'Jews' and the 'Samaritans'."* Rivalry indeed!

The men who would make the committee were as follows:-

Representing the Welfare Committee
Dr Sinclair, The Cottage, Crosshill.
Mr G. Beattie, DCI Buildings, Lochore.
Mr Thomson, The School House, Ballingry.
Mr G. Hutchison, Lochore House, Lochore.
Mr T. Monaghan, Mucklestane Cottage, Crosshill.
Mr W. Crane, Ivanhoe Avenue, Lochore.

Representing the Institute Members
Mr R. Penman, Thelma Cottages, Crosshill.
Mr A. Sinclair, Thelma Cottages, Crosshill.
Mr P. Dignan, Montrose Street, Lochore.
Mr W. McGirr, McGinlay Terrace, Lochore.
Mr W. Duffy, Waverley Street, Lochore.
Mr. D. Martin, Oliver Street, Lochore.

The Officials appointed were
CHAIRMAN — G. Hutchison
VICE CHAIRMAN — R. Penman
TREASURER — A. Sinclair
SECRETARY — D. Martin

To list all the various committees that have served in the years since 1934 would, of course, be impractical, but the authors felt that it would be appropriate, on these pages to list the names of those members who make up the present-day committee.

These are
G. Davie — President
G. Bauld — Secretary
J. Ritchie — Treasurer
A. Marr, A. Payne, A. Johnstone, R. Gibson, D. Drylie, J. Campbell, W. Miller, R. Campbell, G. Gibson

Over the years, of course, Lochore Miners' Social Club, as it is now named, has been the focal point of activity for the people of that village and others who travel from elsewhere to enjoy its excellent facilities.

In common with other Miners' Institutes, it was the venue for meetings, dances, weddings, old folk's 'treats', concerts and other recreational activities, too numerous to mention in any detail. It is to the credit of successive committees that the Lochore Miners Social Club is recognised as one of the most successful in Fife, if not in Scotland, and continues to prosper, even in these difficult times, when unemployment is high and money is short.

Lochore Miners' Welfare
Society and Social Club

Extract of minute of Meeting held on Wednesday 22nd August 1934 to consider the programme for the official opening ceremony of the New Institute on Saturday 15th September, 1934.

Members Present: Mr G. Hutchison, Dr Sinclair, Mr W. Duffy, Mr D. Moffat, Mr A. Sinclair, Mr P. Dignan, Mr G. Beattie, Mr D. Martin.

The following programme was unanimously agreed to:-
1. Mr G. Hutchison to occupy the Chair.
2. Dr Sinclair to accept custody of the New Institute on behalf of the Committee and Community.
3. Mr R. Penman, Vice-Convenor to give a few remarks.
4. Mr K. McNeil, Colliery Agent to give a few remarks.
5. Mr G. Beattie, Finance Convener to move vote of thanks.
6. A vocal and instrumental party would be arranged.
7. A Dance would be held from 7.00 p.m. to 12 midnight and admission would be 9d. for ladies and gents 1/-.

Extracts of Minute of Meeting held on Wednesday 29th August 1934 to draw up a list of people for invitation to the opening ceremony of the New Institute.

Members Present: Mr W. Crane, Mr G. Beattie, Mr A. Sinclair, Mr D. Moffat, Mr G. Hutchison, Mr W. Duffy, Mr D. Martin.

The Secretary submitted a lengthy list of names included in which were the names of all known Secretaries of the various local organisations and also prominent member of the community, also Ladies and Gentlemen who had left the district within the last few years and still had an interest in the social welfare of the inhabitants of the district. After the list had been added to with some other names by the various Members of the Committee, it was unanimously agreed to leave the final adjustments in the power of the Chairman and Secretary.

Minutes of Meeting relating to opening of New Institute.

· CHAPTER 10 ·

Playing The Game

While the Institutes formed the hub of the Social activities within the community in the early days, they were by no means the only source of recreation. Other forms of sports and pastimes were enjoyed by miners and their families. One favourite, amongst mining communities in particular, was whippet racing and many a pound changed hands as a result of one race or another. It was every enthusiast's dream to own a winner, and many an hour was spent training the dogs. Champion dogs were hard to come by and some people would go to great lengths to get a *'winner'* sometimes to be bitterly disappointed. A story worth relating concerns one such whippet, a dog called *'Sunday Post'*. It seems that the Conroy brothers, Tam and Jock, had bought the dog over in the West of Scotland, reputed to be a real *'flyer'*.

'Sunday Post' was exceptionally large for a whippet. Not only that, it was an aggressive, savage brute of a dog — a fact that its previous owners had, not surprisingly, omitted to tell the Conroy brothers! The usual method of whippet running is for someone to hold the dog firmly, until the signal to release the animal is given. As no one has so far been able to hold *'Sunday Post'* without having a hand ripped open by the beast's teeth, it soon became obvious to one and all that the Conroys' dog was a liability — in short , they had been sold a *'pup'*, in more ways than one. Tam Conroy had been bemoaning this fact to all and sundry outside the *'Goth'* one Saturday night, when big Dan Guff overheard.

Dan and his brother Pat, a pair of Irishmen whose brogue was as broad as the boglands of their birth, were well known throughout the area for their love of a good fight now and again, usually after closing time at the *'Goth'*! Anyway, Dan says to Tam Conroy, *"Go get yer dog, Tam, and bejesus! I'll slip it!"* So there was big Dan Guff, grimly holding onto *'Sunday Post'*, while Tam Conroy went along the avenue. About 200 yards or so, took out his handkerchief, and dropped it, in the time honoured method, by which the handler knows to release the dog, who will then run to the *'hankie'*. Tom dropped the hankie, Dan released the dog and, to everyone watching's amazement, *'Sunday Post'* dropped dead at Dan's feet.

It seems that, with the combination of too much drink, and his own incredible strength, Dan had held the whippet too tightly, and had strangled it!

As well as the dogs, and pigeon racing which went on, other forms of gambling were popular, even though, for the most part, they were *'frowned on'* by the more *'respectable'* members of society. *'Pitch and toss'* games were to be found on most weekends, gathering large crowds, especially on a Sunday. More so if there was a good deal of money riding on the eventual outcome of the game.

In the early days, quoits were played, and indeed often produced players as good as anywhere in the land. Many a local lad became quite a celebrity due to his skill and expertise in the game. North Glencraig had its own quoiting stadium. Completely surrounded by corrugated iron fence, some six feet high, the stadium had a pay-stall and a steel rope fence around the arena, to separate the players from the spectators, of which there were many. This old game seems to have disappeared completely now. There was an attempt at one time to revive the game of quoits in Glencraig, but this was short-lived, unfortunately.

More physical pursuits attracted others. Football, golf and athletics have all had a long and proud history throughout the district, and produced sportsmen who, in their day, became household names, not just here, but all over Scotland and beyond.

Football

Football occupied a special place in the hearts of many people in those far off days before the First World War. Teams like Glencraig Celtic, mentioned earlier, helped give their community a sense of identity, just as other sides would do in the years to come.

To become a professional footballer was the dream of many a young man in the mining villages. If nothing else, it offered an escape from the pit. One of those who *'made it'* was **Arthur McGachie**.

Looking back at Arthur's thoughts as a 14 year old boy going down the pit for the first time, one can understand just why he considered himself fortunate.

"My first journey down the pit was very exciting. I wasn't afraid, nor was I apprehensive, but I did wonder what was ahead of me. I collected my lamp and token with my number on it, which I gave to the Banksman, and I followed the rest of the miners into the cage — I had worked on the pithead for a year before this, so I was fully aware of the procedures. Once the cage is filled with the 16 miners, the signal is given and the cage begins its decent. The first thing

that happens is that you become acutely aware of the change in atmosphere. The air feels different, there's a pungent smell and it starts to get warmer the lower you go. After not too smooth a journey, eventually we reach the bottom of the Pit. I remember being totally amazed at what I saw there. The pit bottom is covered in lights along the entire length of the huge arched tunnel. At twenty feet high and sixteen feet wide, it resembles a great hall, whitewashed with bright light.

I remember there were ten hutch tracks, running the full length of the pit bottom, after about a hundred yards or so, these merged into a four tracked roadway where the archway narrowed to about nine feet by seven feet. This was known as the circle girdered archway.

Underground, the coal face was split into separate working sections. My section was number 11 — I was only pleased that it wasn't number 13! We walked for about a half a mile until we came to our section and I saw the coal face for the first time. It's only three feet high and to me it seems very bright and solid, indeed, I found it very hot at the coal face, almost unbearable so, even before I started working I was sweating.

I was told to shovel one of the piles of coal nearer to the hutch and then to fill the hutch with it. By this time I was covered in sweat and dust which seemed to be everywhere. Then I looked over at the other men and discovered they had stripped off most of their clothing and were working in shorts, socks and boots! I had to fill 14 hutches of coal — about 7 tons — and also I had to help make the working area safe by putting in the pit props that supported the roof above us.

Anyway, between casting coal and shoving hutches, as well as transporting full ones out and empty ones in, I soon became completely exhausted. Nobody seemed to have a watch and you had no way of finding out the time, until someone would chalk it up on an incoming hutch for you.

By the end of that first shift underground I was tired and aching from all the scratches over my body, yet very pleased that I had completed a shift at the coal face. I vowed that tomorrow I'd have my shorts and socks, and a 'right pair of Tacketty Boots' — that's if I could make it down here for another day!

Over the course of the next few days, the work did seem to get easier, but I always felt that this was not a job I would choose to do if there was any other work available outside the coal mines".

Fortunately, Arthur had the talent, and the desire, to make that choice.

Reflecting on his career, **Arthur** recalls:

"I just loved to take part in sport, particularly football. I would be quite happy just to be fit and well, and be asked or invited to play. I'd play anywhere, without payment.

In the early 1920s, any club could have me. If I was playing in the team, that was all I would need. I would mix in any game, no matter what the weather was like. No games were ever cancelled in those days — football clubs needed cash coming in every week. On winter afternoons the game would kick off at 2.00, or 2.15 pm — there was no such thing as floodlighting in those far-off days.

Players had to make all their own travelling arrangements as well, and had to buy their rail tickets themselves, claiming their expenses back later, normally after the match.

I gave up playing Junior Football because of the difficulties the clubs experienced in raising enough cash. People talk about the very hard times in the 1930s, but I know from experience that times were more than just hard in the 1920s — almost impossible, in fact. One of the new junior clubs, Crossgates Primrose, were starting up and had heard that I had given up playing football two years earlier. They invited me to play for them, and promised to pay me when circumstances improved. I told them I would play for them, but that I didn't want payment. At that time they were offering players' wages of 7/6d (37½p) per week. While with Primrose, I had trials for East Fife (twice), Hearts, Alloa, Preston North End and Sunderland.

I was very friendly with Johnny Thomson, Celtic's international goalkeeper, and he told me that he received a signing on fee of £10, when he joined Celtic. You can imaging how I felt when East Fife offered me £25 to sign for them — of course I had to accept it!

I had many happy years playing for East Fife, and I remember the many friends I made whilst at Methil. I'm very pleased to say that, even now, sixty years later, some people still remember me.

In July, 1933, after six years at Bayview, I was offered terms to re-sign or, if I wanted, I could accept a 'free transfer', and consider signing-on terms with some other clubs. Dave McLean, the East Fife manager, assured me that 'certain' clubs were making enquiries regarding the situation.

Well, the outcome was that I signed for Dunfermline. I wasn't too pleased with what they were offering, but at least it was near to home, not too far to travel, which was very important back in the 1930s. My impression of East End Park, after only a week there, was that I was 'not going to be staying here long!'.

Dunfermline F.C. had other interests in those days — greyhound racing, etc. Many afternoons and evenings we (the players) could not get training, and at nights the dogs would be attended to in the stripping rooms!

I told the manager, Mr Knight, how I felt about everything, and he said that I could put my transfer request to the Board meeting.

Just before signing for Dunfermline, I had been offered terms by Cowdenbeath F.C. What was very important to me was that these were all local clubs that knew everything about me, and I was very happy to be aware of their interest. So news was passed on about my position at Dunfermline, and on the 27th January, 1934, I was transferred to Cowdenbeath, by their manager Mr William Paterson who had himself been a centre forward with Cowdenbeath.

In the season that I signed for them, Cowdenbeath were in the First Division, the top Scottish League division of the time. Sadly, we were relegated, but at least Dunfermline won promotion that season, so I didn't feel too bad. Whilst playing for Dunfermline, in a Second Division match against Stenhousemuir, we beat them 10-1. This game holds some of my happiest memories for my time at Dunfermline. I scored four goals that day — a day to remember!

The season that ended with Cowdenbeath's relegation to the Second Division, I was placed on the transfer list. Cash was in short supply, so, when a club wrote to me and enquired about what was going to happen, I would be getting a 'free', which is eventually what happened.

I signed for Kings Park (now known as Stirling Albion), but before too long I was on my way again, this time to Leith Athletic, who were currently top of the Second Division. By this time I was in my thirties, and I felt I must make some final decisions about my future, so I started work at the Mary Colliery, which meant I had a steady job with good enough wages, whilst I still continued to play Second Division football with Leith Athletic.

I have many happy memories from my playing career over the years. I well remember running on to the Parkhead pitch, against Glasgow Celtic, and I had to keep telling myself 'You're playing the team that won the League and the Scottish Cup!'

How I loved the West of Scotland supporters! They are the most knowledgeable football fans in the world, and the most loyal. They let their own team — and the opposition — know that, during the whole ninety minutes".

Amongst the other outstanding players who came from the area were Harry Muir*, who played for Glasgow Rangers at the end of the First World War

Footnote: * Harry's grandson, Gary Paterson, joined Dundee this season from Lochore Welfare, keeping up the family tradition.

and his brother Jim, who was on the playing staff at Raith Rovers in the 1920s. Davie Pratt, John McFarlane and Eddie Gilfeather appeared in the famous hooped jersey of Glasgow Celtic all through the 1920s. Gilfeather went on to play for Hibernian before his playing days ended. Bobby Woods of Falkirk and Billy McAndrew incidentally were both killed in the pits.

Ballingry High School produced several outstanding footballers over the years. Alf Melville, who was capped at schoolboy level against both England and Wales in 1925 and who, along with Alex King, were the only two international team members to be chosen from the school at the same time.

In the game against England in 1925, the Scots youngsters were trailing by two goals to one, with less than three minutes of the match remaining, when T. Douglas of Ayr snatched an equaliser. In the dying seconds little Alex King from Ballingry School popped up to score a dramatic winner. In the Gala Parade of 1925, Alex and Alf were publicly honoured and paraded around the streets in a horse-drawn carriage.

Other ex-pupils who went on to become professional footballers included Doug Rougvie, who won every domestic honour in the game during his long spell with Aberdeen F.C. as well as collecting a European medal when the Dons won the Cup Winners Cup in 1983.

Joe and Sandy White, twins who played for Dundee United in the 1960s, George Whisker of Dundee United, and Montrose, Jim and Brian Menzies of Raith Rovers, and amongst others, Robert Morris who went on to play for East Fife and Forfar.

As well as these players, there were others who brought distinction to the area. For example Alex ('Toe') McIntosh played for Wolverhampton Wonderers against Portsmouth in the 1939 English Cup Final. And even greater success was achieved by John Aird, from Glencraig, who was 'capped' for Scotland, whilst a Burnley player, in the 1952 World Cup series.

In addition to those already mentioned there were others who made a successful career in the game through the local junior clubs. The most prominent of all these was Lochore Welfare F.C. At one time they could boast regular crowds of between three and four thousand at their matches. Their honours list makes impressive reading:-

> **League Champions** in 1938-39, 1947-48, 1953-54, 1955-56, 1961-62, 1962-63, 1963-64.
>
> **Fife Cup Winners** in 1937-38, 1950-51, 1961-62, 1963-64, 1979-80.
>
> **Cowdenbeath Cup Winners** in 1952-53, 1955-56, 1961-62, 1963-64, 1967-68, 1974-75.

Lochore Welfare F.C.

The club was formed in 1934, and during its lifetime produced many fine players, too numerous to name, who moved on to play at the highest level of the game, with some of the country's leading clubs. Probably the most outstanding of all of these (ask anyone who saw them!) were men like Jimmy Logie who eventually played for Arsenal, Willie 'Bud' Johnston of Glasgow Rangers, and currently, one of the best players in the country — Craig Levein who played for Cowdenbeath, before moving on to Hearts. All three men played regularly for their country.

Clubs such as Lochore Welfare, popular as they are within the local community are, by necessity, run virtually on a 'shoestring' budget, and require dedicated and hard working committees, in their constant uphill struggle for survival. Finances are always limited and the club relies heavily on unpaid, voluntary assistance. An example of this must surely be the manner in which the club's pavilion was built in the late 1970s. Over 30,000 used bricks were transferred from the recently demolished Nairns factory in Kirkcaldy. Volunteers then hand-cleaned every brick, and the building work was carried out by a few local tradesmen and members of the committee! The task was complete by 1980 and the chairman of the Scottish Sports Council, Peter Heatley, a former Olympic champion, officially opened the new pavilion. With the assistance of Mr Harry Ewing MP, the club managed to reclaim part of the costs for this work.

Golf

On the 1st July, 1908, the '**Dunfermline Echo**' announced the "Formation of a new Golf Course"*

'At a meeting in the Mission Hall, Glencraig, it was decided that a Golf Course would be formed at Glencraig.

A committee was elected as follows:-

> **Hon. Presidents** — *Mr W.H. Telfer and Dr Arnott Dickson.*
>
> **President** — *J. Park,* **Vice-President** — *Dr. Todd*
>
> **Secretary** — *W. Davidson,* **Treasurer** — *J. Duncan*
>
> **Committee Members** — *C. Barclay, D. McChesney, J. Bauld Jnr., T. Plank, J. Melville and Miss Geddes.*

The new course is to be sited east of Glencraig House, between the River Ore and the Mineral Railway, and will be ready to play in a week!'.

At the opening of the course it was 'proposed to hold an exhibition match, with several scratch players from Lochgelly and Cowdenbeath Golf clubs expected to take part'. Sure enough, one week later, on the 8th July, the new course was formally opened! (Its condition can only be imagined).

However, despite that on the 1st August, 1908 in Crosshill the initial steps were taken which would lead, eventually, to the formation of the 'Ballingry Golf Club'. Mr J.F. Park, the school's headmaster held the office of President, from the commencement of the club, right up until 1932 when he left the district. Both he and his wife were made Honorary Members.

In October 1908, it was agreed by the Committee to give up the existing course and approach a local farmer to secure suitable ground for a new golf course. The ground was obtained on the Old Loan East of the River Ore, on a rental basis. A golfing professional, Mr R. Binnie, was engaged to plan the new course, for which he was paid the princely sum of £1. 10/-, plus 4/-d. expenses. The new course opened on the 21st April, 1908.

In November of that year, a Clubhouse, costing £10, and a mower, which cost £6, were brought for the club from the nearby Cowdenbeath Golf Club. In 1910 Ballingry Golf Club joined the West of Fife League. Not content merely to 'rest on their laurels', the club agreed, in August 1911, to rent two more fields at the Old Loan (Torres Loan) from Sir John Wilson, of the Wilson and Clyde Coal Company, on which they proposed to build another new course. Work was started immediately and the new course

Footnote: * Actually, golf had been played in the area many years ago at a site on Benarty Hill, but this had ceased long before this decision was made.

was opened the following April, 1912. Yearly rental would cost the Club £20, but the committee managed to secure £14 of this by renting out the land for grazing purposes! Mr Binnie, who once again, had designed the new course, was paid a fee of £2. 2/-.

The Great War came, and, along with all other forms of sport nationwide, the Golf Club found that the war effected it badly. Funds were low and membership numbers fell drastically. In 1915 it was agreed that any club member serving with the Colours would be retained on the membership for the duration of the hostilities. By 1917, it was agreed that only a part of the course would be utilised — namely, holes no. 1, 2, 3, 4, 5 and 9.

The war eventually dragged to an end, and gradually life began to return to normal, and thoughts turned once more to the pursuit of leisure. In March 1919, a General Meeting was held, to consider the advisability of restarting the club, and it was agreed at that meeting to do so. An interim committee was formed and the meeting was adjourned until after the course would be re-opened, on May 22nd, 1919.

The adjourned A.G.M. was held on that day at the ninth green and a more permanent committee was elected. Membership rose steadily once more, and by the following year plans were in progress for the extension of the clubhouse, in order to provide suitable amenities and accommodation for the growing number of lady members. In that same year, 1920, the Club joined the West Fife Golfing Association. Membership of the Fife Golfing Association and the Golf Union were to follow in 1921.

The Ballingry Golf Club had its roots firmly set in the mining community it was born in and the ups and down of the coal industry affected the club accordingly. During the Miners' Strike of 1921, for instance, the committee passed a motion whereby any Club member on strike could retain his membership on the written promise that they pay after the strike was over.

The General Strike of 1926 affected the Club very badly and the following season showed a deficit in funds of £5.18.8d. Perhaps this is not surprising; too many people had trouble enough feeding and clothing their families without any money, to bother about paying golf club fees!

Nevertheless the Club 'soldiered' on. During the next few years it was a matter of rebuilding the membership and funds. By 1930, membership had risen to 118, on a course on which the Standard Scratch Score had been fixed by the National Union at 65 in 1926.

It was decided in 1933 to try and obtain a new clubhouse. No Gents competitions were held in '33 or '34; instead, all monies were being channelled into the efforts to get the new clubhouse. The effort proved worthy, and a new pavilion was purchased and was opened on 19th June, 1935.

The Second World War had a devastating effect on the club. In 1940 it was reluctantly decided not to engage a Greenkeeper, all work on the course being undertaken voluntarily by the members themselves. Things, unfortunately, did not improve. In 1941 it was decided not to run the Club that year, due to the scarcity of members. In June, the Ministry of Supply approached the Club, with a view to renting part of the course, in order to stack quantities of pit wood. The committee agreed to sub-let part of their ground to the Ministry. This brought in some money, but not enough to save the Pavilion, which the Club sold off in February 1942, for £150. The following month, the Club asked to be released from its tenancy of the Golf Club, and this was agreed, as of 28th May. The money left in the Club's funds — £120 — was invested in Defence Bonds, and a committee was organised to look after these.

After the war, a few attempts were made to restart the Club and also to obtain ground for a new course, but all these efforts were in vain.

During its lifetime, the original Ballingry Golf Club had only two Presidents. Mr J. F. Park, one of the men responsible for the club's formation, and Charles Barclay, a founder member of the 1908 committee. Charles Barclay was Club Captain between 1909 and 1911, became Secretary in 1912, a post he held until 1929, and Vice President in 1931. He took over the Presidency in 1932 and remained in that capacity until 1952. Mr Barclay was made an Honorary Member in 1929. A local Schoolteacher, Miss Storrie, became an Honorary Member in 1934.

A Public Meeting in August 1971 decided to restart Ballingry Golf Club, and to try to get ground for a new course. After three years of negotiations with various bodies, both the local Council and Fife County Council agreed the plans for a new course. However, the application for a grant from the Scottish Sports Council was unsuccessful, and a private course was not feasible. Further meetings with the local and Fife Councils were asked for, but did not materialise.

Finally, in 1976, the new Dunfermline District Council and the Fife Regional Council were asked to consider building a Municipal Golf Course in the area. This they eventually agreed to and a new Course was constructed at the Lochore Country Park. It opened for play on 25 April 1981, and the Clubhouse is a room in the park centre. In 1983 the course was supplied

Roll of Honour
BALLINGRY GOLF CLUB

Captains		Champions	
1909	Charles Barclay	1911	William Davidson
1910	Charles Barclay	1912	James Melville
1911	Charles Barclay	1913	John Morris
1912	William Davidson	1914	James Bauld
1913	John Morris	1915	NOT PLAYED
1914	John Morris	1916	James Bauld
1915	John Morris	1917	James Bauld
1916	John Morris	1918	John Bauld
1917	John Morris	1919	John Ferguson
1918	John Morris	1920	James Ross
1919	John Morris	1921	William Andrew
1920	Hugh Coulter	1922	Lawrie Anderson
1921	Hugh Coulter	1923	Wiliam Stark
1922	Hugh Coulter	1924	NOT PLAYED
1923	John Morris	1925	Lawrie Anderson
1924	Alex Steele	1926	NOT PLAYED
1925	Alex Steele	1927	NOT PLAYED
1926	Hugh Coulter	1928	Alex Butters
1927	John Morris	1929	William Andrew
1928	Murdoch Stuart	1930	NOT PLAYED
1929	William Stark	1931	William Herd
1930	William Andrew	1932	James Clark
1931	William Andrew	1933	NOT PLAYED
1932	James Ferguson	1934	NOT PLAYED
1933	James Ferguson	1935	Robert Herd
1934	James Ferguson	1936	Malcolm Duncan
1935	James Ferguson	1937	John Steele
1936	Walter C. Howat	1938	James Jackson
1937	James Watson	1939/42	NOT PLAYED
1938	James Watson		
1939	John Steele	1981	Brian Duffy
1940	John Steele	1982	Thomas Easton
1941	John Steele	1983	Thomas Easton
1942	John Steele	1984	Simon Wilson
		1985	Michael Sanaghan
1981-82	John Murphy	1986	Ian Davidson
1983-84	William Glencross	1987	Thomas Easton
1985-86	John Murphy	1988	Ian Davidson
1987-88	Robertson Davidson	1989	Thomas Easton
1989	John Murphy	1990	Terry Ironside
1990-91	Michael Connolly	1991	Terry Ironside
1992	Peter Park	1992	James J. Morris

Honorary Members of the Club are Douglas Johnstone, John Murphy, Jim Mackie, Willie Clarke and Tom McPhillips.

with its own watering system. During the 1984 Miners' Strike, as in the 1926 Strike, it was once more agreed that any member on strike could have full membership on agreement that they pay after the strike.

Since Ballingry Golf Club was opened at Lochore Meadows in 1981 it has produced several good young players. The following are those who have represented Fife at Boys' levels:-

Michael Sanaghan — 1983, 1984, 1985, 1986
Craig Kidd — 1986
Stephen Payne — 1985, 1986
Ian McLeod — 1985
Terry Ironside — 1986, 1987
Colin Fraser — 1989
Alan Mackie — 1990, 1992
Paul Wheatley — 1992

Those who went on to represent the 'Kingdom' at Youth Level are:-

Michael Sanaghan, Terry Ironside, Stephen Payne and Paul Marwick.

The success that the young golfers have achieved augurs well for the future of Ballingry Golf Club and brings credit to the area.

Athletics

There is no doubt that athletics has long proved to be a popular pastime for several generations of Benarty folk. In the pre-war years, the local children loved nothing better than when some of the older teenagers, and there, on the 440 yard track made by pedestrians on the dune hills, they put the kids 'through their paces', in preparation for the Gala Day Races.

There had been a history of professional runners in the area. In 1924, for example, the Powderhall half-mile was won by a Glencraig man — W. Howard. Years later, a newspaper article (published in the 1960s) paid tribute to the districts' runners under the heading 'Ballingry and Pedestrianism'. The article said,

"The Ballingry, Lochore and Crosshill district has a record of pedestrianism which will be hard to equal in Scotland or the North of England, the areas most concerned with the main events of the year — the New Year handicaps at Powderhall.

For the last six successive years, there has been a local athlete in the prize-lists. Here is the list:-

1963: D. Campbell, Ballingry — second in the sprint.
1964: W. Duncan, Ballingry — first in the mile.
1965: W. Duffy, Ballingry — fourth in the half mile.
1966: W. Duffy, Ballingry — second in the half mile.
1967: J. Salmond, Ballingry — second in the mile.
1968: J. McGowan, Ballingry — first in the half mile.

This is an impressive list and it is even more interesting to note that all six 'peds' were trained by the same man — Mr Harry Hutchison, a former pedestrian, who ran under H. Hutchison, Kinross, before the last war. The training sessions were, and still are, held in the local playing field at Crosshill.

D. Campbell also ran third in the 1967 Powderhall Sprint, and for this he was trained by J.G. Sharkey, Cowdenbeath. Also to be taken into account for the district is the performance of the Rutherford brothers from Ballingry. Robert has many wins to his credit at various games meetings; Harry, a sterling performer and Powderhall gold medal winner under A. Mitchell, Kelty; and Willie, an outstanding athlete who set up a record by winning the Jedburgh £150 handicap for two years in succession (Willie was trained by J. Bradley, Edinburgh).

Other prominent winners who spring to mind are J. Menzies, Crosshill, J. Baird, Lochore, who has been figuring in prize-lists for the past twenty-one years, and is still competing; and G. Erskine, Lochore. Also W. Brown, Glencraig and Danny 'Gallacher' (Marshall), Glencraig trained by W. Brown, who won a Powderhall Summer Handicap. They all contributed to making the Ballingry area one of the top districts in Scotland, and beyond the border, as far as pedestrianism is concerned.''

Highland Games

As well as these athletics, Ballingry had its own Highland Games for a period, attracting some of the biggest names in Athletics and other sports, as well as providing top quality entertainment for the crowds who flocked to the games.

Harry Hutchison, one of the founder members of the Highland Games Committee recalls how it all came about,

"On the 10th April, 1949, a meeting was held in Lochore Institute of various bodies, along with members of the public, who were interested in forming a

committee to get a local Highland Games organised. Amongst those represented at this meeting were the Lochore Institute, the Lochore Pipe Band, the children's Gala Committee and Lochore F.C., as well as several members of the general public.

Councillor David Martin spoke first. He gave details of a scheme which had been run successfully during the war years — 'Holidays At Home' — which had comprised of Socials, dances and Sports day etc. from which quite a bit of money had accrued, and Councillor Martin was very keen to use that money to start up a Highland Gathering that would be worthy of this area".

The outcome of the meeting that night, was the formation of a Games Committee and the setting of a date and place for the first Highland Games. The committee officials, appointed at that time, were Edward McCann as Chairman, John Murphy as Secretary, and Harry Hutchison who took over the duties of Treasurer. David Martin was voted on to the committee along with Messrs Leishman, Nelson, Gibbon, Marr, Carr and Mackie.

The date set for the first Games was Saturday, August 20th, 1949, and the venue would be Central Park, Crosshill.

Harry Hutchison again,

"The Games were run annually for six years, more or less successfully. Athletes such as Barney Ewell, who won a silver medal at the 1948 Olympics in London, in the 220 metres event and the Australians, Cummings and Andrews, Powderhall Sprint winners were brought here — for a fee, of course!

We had our little difficulties, naturally, in finding the necessary money. When Barney Ewell appeared someone mentioned that if we had a bad day, with a poor turnout, we could be struggling to pay for him. The Secretary reported that, of course, we would pay the man, even if it had to be in instalments!

As it happened, Ewell did appear, but he refused to run in the Sprint, saying that the track was too bad. The track was in the field at the back of Ballingry School, and to be honest, it was a bit rough, to say the least. The Athlete was obviously worried about injuring himself, but he did agree to run in the 220 yards event. Anyway, we had a fine day and Ewell was paid at the end of it, after all!

We had similar problems with Cummings, who also protested that the running track was too rough. That time the track was in the fields where Rosewell Drive is nowadays.

Then there was the Glasgow hotel lad who was going to send on a cheque he

LOCHORE AND CROSSHILL HIGHLAND GAMES

Financial Statement for 1951

INCOME		£	s	d
Brought Forward	...	157	3	7
Dancing run in Institute	...	27	0	0
Crosshill Tavern	...	5	0	0
Lochore Gothenburg	...	10	0	0
Stalls and Sale of Programmes	...	28	7	6
Carpark and Circle Seats	...	7	18	9
Gate Money	...	122	19	0
Entry Fees and Showmen	...	16	11	0
Interest	...	1	15	8
Caterers	...	10	0	0
		£ 386	15	6

EXPENDITURE		£	s	d
Honorariums (1950)	...	15	0	0
Police	...	8	11	0
Prizes to Competitors	...	114	0	0
Advertising and Printing	...	24	14	0
Loud Speaker Van	...	5	5	0
Secretary's Expenses	...	4	0	0
Donation to Scouts	...	1	0	0
Eric Cummings	...	22	0	0
Dance Band and Hire of Halls	...	30	3	0
Judges' Fees and Games Assistants' Fees	...	5	5	0
Richard Masterton	...	4	0	0
Car Hires, Starting Blocks, etc.	...	5	10	0
Caterers	...	24	6	6
Gate Attendants & Games Ass. Meetings	...	7	0	0
		£ 270	14	6
In Bank	...	116	1	0
		£ 386	15	6

We, the undersigned, having gone over the Books, Receipts and Bank Book of the above find them in good order, and as hereby stated

DAVID MARTIN
GEORGE ARMSTRONG Auditors.

Edward McCann, President; J. M. Murphy, Secretary; H. Hutchison, Treasurer *owed us, for having the rights to the Beer Tent. After a week or two, when no cheque had appeared, we made enquiries only to discover his business had been sequestrated, and he had beat it to Ireland! Simpson was his name.*

Crosshill playpark was an ideal venue for the Games, but unfortunately we were only allowed to use it on one occasion. The Games were eventually abandoned in 1955, owing in part, to the lack of suitable arenas, which contributed greatly to the general lack of support".

A Financial Statement, for the year 1951 is printed in this book, showing the expenditure and income from the Lochore and Crosshill Highland Games.

Cricket

The game of cricket is not generally thought of as being one normally associated with mining areas, yet Crosshill Cricket Club has flourished for well over sixty years. Ironically, the club was a by-product of the 1926 Miners Strike!

During the Strike, some of the miners felt that even with all their strike duties — collecting for the soup kitchen, picketing the colliery gates etc, they still had too much time on their hands and they decided to do something about this. The result was the formation of Crosshill C.C.

With the help of Andrew Crowe, Glencraig's manager, who had always expressed an interest in trying to get a cricket club started in the district, the men managed to get the use of a piece of rough ground from Sir John Wilson. The ground was indeed very rough, covered in large rocks and boulders, but once more, Andrew Crowe helped out, arranging for ammunition from the pit to be used to blast out the rocks, as well as supplying lengths of bogey-rails and bogeys themselves to transport materials for completing the cricket pitch. This must surely have been one of the more unusual examples of worker-management co-operation during the Strike!

When the pitch was completed, Dunfermline Cricket Club were invited along to play Crosshill on the official opening day. Several members of the Dunfermline club also helped to coach the Crosshill team and trained them in the days leading up to Crosshill's membership of the local Cricket League.

Once King George V Playing field was established in 1938 it was agreed that Crosshill Cricket Club would have the right to play their matches there for as long as they required. Thankfully, for the club still operates in the area. Quite an achievement for a few striking miners in 1926.

Crosshill Cricket Club

Cycling

Another hobby-cum-sport that captured the imagination of a great many people in the days between the two World Wars was that of cycling. We are particularly indebted to **Mr James Hamilton** for the following brief history of one such cycle club — The Ballingry Roads Cycling Club

"The club was founded in 1931 by a few young men in the district who liked to get out and about after working a hard shift in the local mines. The most memorable names that come to mind were Tommy Clark, Jimmy Fotheringham, Sammy McGhee, Mick Devine, Chic Seaman, and my own father, Tom Hamilton.

My memory is a bit vague, as I was just a few years old at the time, but what I do remember were the weekends we went to the sports rally in all the Fife Clubs at Burnside and the runs to the Linn at Stanley in Perthshire.

The club was disbanded during the War years, and started up again in 1947-48. By this time I had become a member of Auchterderran Wheelers and was racing in time-trials. As the Ballingry Club was being reformed, I came back and rejoined in 1948.

Ballingry Cycling Club

The club in the 1950s was very strong, with about 90 or so members, about 60 or so of which took an active part in all the club's activities, cycling and socially. I remember about 30 or so members cycling up to Anstruther for a festival, with all our bikes decorated with crepe paper and ribbons, and my father and I taking turns on the 'Penny Farthing' our club had acquired a few years earlier. It was rather difficult to mount, but, once on, it was easy to ride. In the early '50s the club had a good number of members who took part in races. Apart from myself there was Fred Fenton, who went off to Australia, Bobby Martin and Charlie Green, who went to Canada, Jim Green, Ken Geddes, Jackie Scott, Jimmy McGhee, Peter Grant (the club chairman) and Jimmy and Davie Murphy to name but a few.

The club also had a number of women members — June Green, the Geddes sisters, the Fenton sisters and Mima Greenless, all of whom helped in some way to make the club an enjoyable place to spend an evening. We used to meet in the Flockhouse Hall, which sadly, is no longer there, but I'm sure even the mention of its name will bring back some fond memories for many members of those bygone days. The club also attracted a few outsiders through the years, people such as Walter Willshire, from Glenfarg, and Mr and Mrs Brown from Cowdenbeath.

The Ballingry Club's members were especially active when there was an interclub sports day. One such rally that I remember well, was the one at Auchtertool,

126

when we beat Dunfermline and district to win the Sports Shield, which was competed for every year. I think we won that trophy three years in a row.

Unfortunately, like so many other things from the past, the club eventually collapsed, with all the trophies that our members competed for over the years being donated to the Fife Cyclist Association. Now, alas, the Ballingry Roads Cycling Club exists only as a fond memory for those who were one-time members".

Footnote: There were, of course, other sports which took place over the years, such as boxing, but unfortunately, we could not gather sufficient information to do them justice.

· CHAPTER 11 ·

The Last Great Strike

Whilst the closure of the Mary and Glencraig Pits in 1966 effectively ended coal mining in the Benarty area itself (except for the open cast site at Westfield), nevertheless the villages were still regarded as mining communities. Although a number of families had moved to the more prosperous coalfields in England, most of the miners who remained in the industry found employment in the remaining Fife pits and travelled there by the pit bus.

The situation continued until the 12 month long miners strike of 1984, the final consequence of which was that not only did Benarty cease to have any significant connection with the mining industry, but indeed the whole of Scotland finally contained only one working colliery at Castlebridge. Two other collieries, Frances at Kirkcaldy and Monktonhall in East Lothian, were kept open on a *'care and maintenance'* basis, in the hope that their unique reserves of low sulphur coal could be exploited later.

Certainly, if Benarty was seen as a mining community up till 1984, the Great Strike finally destroyed that image. And, of course with the magnificent job done by the Fife Regional Council in restoring the landscape from the ravages of its coal mining past, the main feature being the Lochore Meadows Country Park, there were few visible signs of the past.

In that sense the 1984 strike marked the death of the coal industry which had been born a century ago, and had shaped, not only the countryside, but the lives of the families who depended on it for their existence. It was, therefore, of extreme importance in our story and merits some attention.

The history of mining from the days when miners were slaves, and after, when unions were first formed and developed, was a history of conflict and strife. It was littered with strikes, local and national, as miners fought to achieve decent wages and conditions of work.

In fact, this particular strike was the third national strike in twelve years, the others being in 1972 and 1974. However, to those who endured the long 12 month struggle, the first two were described as purely *'skirmishes'*. In both cases they lasted only a few weeks, both were about wage increases, and both resulted in outstanding victories for the miners, with huge wage awards being won. Indeed the 1974 strike resulted in the defeat of the Heath Tory Government, and for many older miners was heralded as revenge at last for the terrible result of the 1926 General Strike, when the miners fought on for seven months, only to return to worse conditions than they had before.

But if the miners enjoyed the euphoria of victory in 1974, the Tories in turn, vowed that never again would they be humiliated in that way, and in the intervening years they prepared the *'Nicholas Ridley Strategy'*, designed to destroy the power of the miners for ever, as prelude to weakening the whole British Trade Union Movement.

That strategy and its vicious pursuit is well documented elsewhere, and for our purposes we want only to look at its effect on the mining community of Benarty.

By 1984 there were only some 300 miners living in the villages which make up Benarty, most of whom were employed at Seafield, some at Frances, and a few at the Cowdenbeath Workshops, a far cry from the 3,000 families who depended on the local pits for their living in their heyday. However, most families had historic connections with mining one way or another, and as in the whole of Scotland, there was massive support for the miners' cause.

It would be true to say that before the strike, there was little enthusiasm for it and it is doubtful if a ballot could have been won.

However, it is equally true that once battle commenced, no effort was to be spared, no sacrifice too great to make, no greater loyalty to their Union and to their fellow miners to be found, than that demonstrated by the men from Fife, whose militancy was legendary dating back to their being the first miners in Europe to win the eight-hour day in 1870.

This strike was not about wages and conditions — it was a struggle to defend the very existence of mining communities, and it would be fought with bitter intensity to the very end.

The local strike centre was Lochore Miners Institute and the Chairman of the strike committee, Ronnie Campbell, who was later victimised for his activities and never re-employed. The Secretary was SNP Councillor for Crosshill, Joe Paterson, and the Treasurer George Bauld. At the Fife area headquarters, Councillor Willie Clarke was joint Chairman and George Davie was joint Secretary, both local men.

During the year long strike there were countless activities — picketing all over Scotland, demonstrations and rallies, organising every possible kind of fund-raising to sustain the mining families, along with the day to day feeding of people in the strike centres. In all of this the Lochore Centre played its part, not least the Women's Action Group who were formed late in May and became a tower of strength throughout the strike, even when some men were beginning to crack. The Chairperson of the Women's Action Group was Mrs Mary Coll and its Secretary was Mrs Betty Guthrie.

Whilst it would be impossible here to recall all that happened in the strike, there were one or two local events that were very special. The first arose out of one of the few successful pickets in Scotland, which was at Cartmore Industrial Site in Lochgelly. An attempt was made by the Coal Board to shift opencast coal from the site to power stations in England. This provoked a mass picket at the site with miners assembling there from Fife and Lothians to try and stop the hated transport company of Yuill and Dodds taking the coal away. Whilst the picket was relatively peaceful, nevertheless the police took a heavy-handed approach, arresting almost anyone who moved, so that in two days 133 pickets had been charged with obstruction. This was the greatest number of arrests at any one picket in Britain, and compared with the two dozen arrests at Orgreave in the most violent picket of the strike, shows how much the police went over the top.

However, the Yuill and Dodds lorries attempted to approach Lochgelly from the back door, which took them through Ballingry. There they were met with great hostility by pensionsers, housewives and youngsters who poured abuse on them at every point along the road. The final straw for the lorry-drivers came when well over 100 youngsters, between the ages of 12 and 14 years, instead of marching into school, marched out on to the road down through the village to Lochore Miners Institute singing and shouting and blocking the way of the worried lorry drivers. After a cup of tea there they marched on for a mile or so and the action of these youngsters added to the mass picketing at the open cast site was too much for the Scab Drivers. They never re-appeared — a victory at last for the pickets.

Another major event was a mass Rally organised by the Women's Action Group during the traditional annual holiday fortnight. It brought together 3,000 miners, their wives and families, from all over Scotland for a day out at Lochore Country Meadows Park. The marchers assembled at Ballingry Social Club at mid-day and marched through the village, with their bands and their banners in a colourful demonstration to the park. There they were entertained throughout the afternoon with speeches, music and song, in a real family picnic atmosphere, a welcome break from the daily grind of the Strike Centre and the picket line, and a fine example of how the women were supporting their menfolk in the struggle.

The strike of course lasted for a long twelve months, although the miners sensed after the *'Battle of Orgreave'* that they could not hope to win, and it became a matter of survival. The drift back to work began after Christmas, but in keeping with the traditional militancy of the Fife miners, 95% of those who went on strike at the start were still out at the end. Life was very difficult for those who broke ranks, as *'scabs'* were despised in the mining communities.

Eventually the strike ended in a bitter defeat for the miners, who returned to work *without a settlement'* and was followed quickly by savage retribution by the Coal Board. Ian McGregor, the Chairman, a figure detested by the miners and their families, had labelled miners as the *'enemy within'* and the Thatcher Government had deployed every possible power and force of the State to crush them. McGregor promised the public that *'the miners would pay the price of insurrection'* and he was as good as his word. Closures, redundancies and victimisation were the order of the day.

Demoralisation ater the strike, the accumulated debts, the sackings, the court charges and the fines all had their effect and the closure plans were pushed through with little resistance. Indeed most men had had enough, they volunteered for redundance en masse and within a few years the Scottish coalfield had shrunk from 13 working pits to only one and the labour force from over 17,000 to around 2,000.

Against this stark picture, the positive features of the strike were the sense of community which developed amongst the people, and the emergence of women as an organised body, finding capacities within themselves that they never knew existed before, all of which was not lost after the strike.

Now, only a handful of miners were left in Benarty, and although, because so many people had been associated with mining in the past, they still identified themselves with mining, the reality was that, after the strike, Benarty effectively ceased to be a mining community. The cycle had been completed.

There was a postcript, however. A Miners Strike Commemoration Committee was formed in 1989 so that there would be a permanent Memorial to the greatest mining strike in British history, and to the mining families who were involved.

On Saturday 6th May, 1989, thousands of those who had been involved, marched, probably for the last time, from Lochore Institute, behind the local Pipe Band, to a rally at the Meadows Park, to an afternoon of speeches, songs and music. The highlight was the unveiling of the Commemoration

1984-5 Strike Commemorative Plaque

Stone by Mick McGahey, the revered former President of the Miners Union in Scotland, who paid tribute to the courage of the miners and their families for their solidarity and support during the strike.

The stone was blessed by the Rev. Hugh Ormiston, a powerful supporter of the miners all through the strike and is now situated outside the centre building. It bears a plaque with the following inscription, *'erected by the Scottish People in recognition of the struggle of the Fife miners and their families during the year long strike 1984-85'*.

It is a fitting testament to the courage and solidarity of those who were involved in that strike, but also for the local people a memorial to that Industry which dominated their lives for over a Century, and ended with this final struggle.

Looking back now, few would have estimated the ultimate price that the miners would pay for their defeat.

All the predictions of the mining leaders about the scale of the closure programme, however exaggerated they seemed at the time, turned out to be an underestimation of the decimation the Industry would suffer. On 13th October 1992 British Coal announced that only 19 pits would be left, after their latest round of closures, with the loss of 30,000 mining jobs and the terrible consequences for those who depended on coal-mining for their living. However, this decision provoked a massive protest and as part of a national campaign 200,000 people marched in pouring rain through London on Sunday 27th October. The reaction shook the Government, who had to re-think their energy policy in the face of the public outcry. The final outcome is not yet known.

This was to be the ultimate cost to the mining communities of that great struggle the miners waged to defend jobs and a way of life, now to be lost not just in Benarty, but throughout all the former coalfields.

· CHAPTER 12 ·

Final Reflections

We have traced the rise and fall of mining in Benarty over the period of a century. It was coal that created the villages of Glencraig, Crosshill and Lochore, with Ballingry built later to provide more modern housing for those who worked in the industry. Without coal these places would never have existed — it was their *'reason for being'*. But not only did coal-mining produce work and wages, it also shaped every aspect of life for those who dwelt in the shadow of the Pit Bing.

Certainly it was the fluctuation in the demand for coal from the Victorian era, through two world wars, the interwar years and the years since, which determined the fortunes of the people who lived here, and though there were periods of relative prosperity, in the main the early days were ones of hard work, poverty and social deprivation for the mining families. Yet within that, an intimate neighbourliness, friendship, an absence of sectarianism, a concern for others, a sense of community among people bonded together by the common features of their work. As men depended on each other underground for their livelihood and their safety, so that bond remained above ground in the streets of their mining villages. Doors could go unlocked; old people, women and children could walk freely without fear. Certainly the miners worked hard, oft-times drunk hard and played hard, but there was an unwritten code of behaviour by which people lived, which unfortunately today seems to be lost.

In the century we have covered the world has changed out of all recognition. The pace of technological advance has been breathtaking when we look back, and the lives of people transformed dramatically. Who would have foreseen 100 years ago that man would go to the moon, the tremendous advances in science and medicine, means of transportation, the wonders of computers, television, film and video?

How could the football supporter who stood in the rain watching Glencraig Celtic ever imagine that one day he would be able to sit in his armchair at home watching the world's best players on a TV set? Or a mining family instead of taking a bus to Burntisland or Leven for a week's holiday, if they could afford such a treat, would one day fly out in a jet plane to the sunny beaches of Spain or Greece? Or people whose travel was confined to a tram-ride to Dunfermline, would drive all over Britain in their own cars, and live in double-glazed, centrally heated houses, with all the latest home appliances, as property owners — truly changed days.

That is not to say, of course, that there is no poverty today, for there is, and it is on a large scale, affecting the young, the unemployed, the sick and elderly. But it is a relative poverty, which cannot be compared with the conditions of sixty years ago. Few would want to return to *'those good old days'*, when life was dominated by the Pit, when almost every boy knew from the day he was born that there would be no other choice for him but to join his father down the pit. Women faced a life of hard work and hardship, often just trying desperately to survive, with large families, where each new born child was often greeted not as a blessing, but yet another mouth to feed.

It is no wonder that this area had its particular political features. It was the aftermath of the First World War, the two great strikes of 1921 and 1926, countless local strikes and demonstrations, the constant struggle against poverty, the Hungry Thirties and Means Test, the dreadful housing conditions and the fight for a better life, which created the fertile ground for the growth of Socialist ideas and the election of Communist and Labour councillors. Indeed the election of the first Communist MP in Britain, Willie Gallacher to represent this area was a result of the struggles of the years from 1919 to 1935.

There were also a number of great miners' leaders who were a product of those days, notably Abe and Alex Moffat, who both became presidents of Scottish Area NUM, and later Lawrence Daly, committed to this socialist tradition, became that union's General Secretary. But apart from these, each of the local pits had its own stalwarts over the years who will be fondly remembered by many miners for their efforts to improve the miners' lot. Credit should also be paid to the numerous councillors, of differing political shades who have represented this area and who sought to improve the quality of life for the families in these villages.

But now things have changed dramatically. One hundred years ago there were just under a million miners. At nationalisation in 1947 over 700,000 were in the pits. Today it is forecast that less than 20,000 will be left in 1993. Coal was once the main source of energy in Britain at the zenith of its power in world affairs with a mighty Empire. Now that Empire is gone, and Britain is becoming a junior partner in Europe. Coal has lost its place, ironically, to other more expensive sources of energy such as oil, gas and nucleur power, a deliberate act by a government determined to defeat the miners who had been the shock-troops of the Trade Union movement.

In Scotland only one working pit remains, Castlebridge on the River Forth feeding Longannet Power Station, with Frances Colliery in mothballs waiting hopefully for a new owner.

The nationalisation which was so welcomed in 1947 by the miners as an escape from the old coal-owners, who treated them badly, is being reversed. The privatisation of the few remaining pits is on the cards, the once mighty Miners Union is split in two, with a small membership and seeking to amalgamate with another more powerful union.

Even the ideas of Socialism, which was seen by many as the answer to the social injustice they suffered in the 20s and 30s, have lost their attraction, with the collapse of the former Soviet Union and Eastern European countries on one hand, and the return of a fourth successive Tory Government, with Labour in disarray, on the other.

In the Benarty area, with its particular political background, there is a mixture of council representation: a Labour District Councillor, Allan Gray; an SNP District Councillor, Joe Paterson; and a Communist Regional Councillor, Willie Clark. This combination, whilst clearly arising from the tradition of the area, also nowadays probably reflects as much the personal qualities of these men, as the current political views of the electors.

So — what now? What future for these villages and the people who live there, many of whom have still vivid memories of the Coal Industry and the lasting impact on their lives? Like so many other mining communities throughout Scotland their *'reason for being'* is gone, with only their memories, and a few memorials and landmarks to remind them of their past and to interest the new generations who will follow. The process of regeneration is beginning, albeit against a background of demoralisation and despair. Improvements to the infrastructure are being made. The Lochore Meadows Country Park reflects the efforts going into the creations of a leisure industry. A fine new secondary school has been built in nearby Lochgelly, recognising the importance placed on good education. Efforts are being made locally to train people in projects like BRAG, to equip them with new skills and make them more self-reliant.

It is unrealistic to expect that some major new industry will suddenly burst upon the scene to solve the unemployment problem, taking up where the coal industry left off. Recovery, if it takes place at all, will be gradual. The fact is that nobody really knows what the future holds, but Councillor Willie Clarke, with typical enthusiasm, senses that the worst is over, and a new confidence and optimism is growing. Perhaps someone in later years will chronicle just how well-founded optimism was.

For those still around who lived in the first half of the 20th century, they will surely look back with mixed feelings on the coal industry. On one hand the grinding work, the dangerous conditions, the poverty and poor housing, the women's drudgery and the accidents and illness that went with the job — none of these will be missed. Indeed most miners never wanted their sons to go down the pit, but for most there was no other option. At least it was a job, and even today it would be preferable to the frustration and depression which goes with unemployment.

On the other hand, there was that identity of purpose, the sense of belonging to a Community, the friendship, the concern for neighbours, a respect for others and the pleasure of social company, much of which has gone today.

It is natural as people grow older that they tend to look more backwards than forwards, and in the group who produced this book, there was a lot of looking back — and talking about events and characters. For example Dr Sinclair, doing his rounds on his bike, Father Mulherran and the Reverend Mason looking after their flocks, *'Bash the Pan'* ringing his bell and Pug Jock with his big flouncy bucket. Or what about *'Kate the Tink'*, Old *'Doc'* Robertson, *'Darkie'* Blythe, the huge family of Agnews *('enough to make a football team')* or Mrs Reddington who read cups. Then the strong men like *'Joe the Pole'*, *'Bear Broon'*, or the Irish brothers Pat and Dan Guff. Who remembers *'Bump'* Holland, Frankie Gibb, Old Johnny Layden or Geordie Morris on Gala Day, Old Pete Campbell, the McCormack brothers or Old Jimmy Moffat? There was Marshall the draughts champion, Gibson the boxer, McGachie the footballer and so on and on. These are but a part of the folklore of Benarty, along with numerous others forming the fabric of life which was created by the discovery of coal. Perhaps someone else can take up the tales that were told about them so that they are not lost for ever, for they are like the coal — part of a rich heritage.

Now this area has been returned to something like its original state in the shade of Benarty Hill. The visible scars of mining have gone but not all of the human ones can be so readily removed. The memories of the past will remain in the minds of those who felt its presence for so long, and hopefully we will not only have stimulated those memories, especially the pleasant ones, but also we hope that we have left something for new generations to come, so that they are aware of their Mining Heritage.

Perhaps the last word should be left to Sir Walter Scott, who was associated with this area, and whose works are commemorated by the street names in Lochore. He wrote this in another context, but is relevant to our theme, as an obituary to the Coal Industry of Benarty:

"Like the dew on the mountain
Like the foam on the river
Like the bubble on the fountain
Thou art gone and forever".

APPENDIX 1

Information About Local Schools

BALLINGRY

The only logs held by the Authority are for Ballingry Public School 1873-1911 and for Ballingry Public School Infant Department 1908-1939.

BALLINGRY PUBLIC SCHOOL

Log opens on 17 October 1873, when the headmaster seems to have been a Mr Keppie, who was declared incompetent by a special inspection on July 1878. After the holidays the school remained closed for 18 weeks, until it was reopened on 30 November, under the charge of a schoolmistress who kept the log but did not identify herself.

On 5 September 1879, a new headmaster, Mr William MacIntosh, took charge, remaining at the school until 9 April 1886.

Mr William Shaw was headmaster from 23 April 1886 until 6 April 1900, when Mr James K. Park was appointed.

Mr Park was still in post at the time of the last log entry in 1911.

BALLINGRY PUBLIC SCHOOL INFANT DEPARTMENT

The Infant Department was opened as a separate unit from the Junior and Senior Division on 6 January 1908 under the charge of Annie B. Robertson.

On 30 September 1909 a new infant school was formally opened by Mr Wilson, Chairman of the Board. The headmistress was a Miss Dunbar, who remained in post until 19 April 1918.

Miss Sorrie was headmistress from 22 April 1918 until 29 March 1934.

Although not explicitly recorded in the log, the text suggests that from 31 August 1934, the head was a Miss Miller, who was still in post at time of the last log entry in 1939.

GLENCRAIG SCHOOL

Opened first on Monday 1 February 1904

Miss Kate C. Philp
Headmistress from 1 February 1904 until retiral on 6 July 1928

Mr Andrew Skene
Headmaster from 28 August 1928 until appointed Headmaster of Dysart 10 July 1936

Mr J. G. Dougary
Headmaster from 11 September 1936 until transfer to military service on 2 May 1941.

Mr John Moffat
Acting Headmaster, 2 May 1941 to 21 May 1945

Mr J.G. Dougary

Resumed duty 21 May 1945 until retiral through ill health in August 1951

Mr James Mailer

Headmaster from 27 August 1951 until appointed Headmaster of Benarty 30 April 1956

Mr John P. Smart

Headmaster from 1 May 1956 until appointed Headmaster of Lumphinnans 23 August 1960

Mr William Halyburton

Depute Headteacher of Benarty seconded as Interim Headmaster from 23 August 1960 until closure of school.

School closed on 2 February 1962.

N.B. Miss Jennie Lee, who became an M.P. taught at this school In the late '20's. She married Aneuran Bevan in 1934 and went on to a long Parliamentary career culminating in being appointed Minister of the Arts.

ST KENNETHS SCHOOL
(formerly Lochore RC School, Glencraig)

Opened first on 13 October 1914

Mrs M. G. Davis

Headmistress from 13 October 1914 until dismissal on 3 May 1915

Miss Catherine McCormick

Headmistress from 3 May 1915 until retiral on 28 February 1933

Miss Bracelin

Interim Headmistress, 1 March 1933 to 26 May 1933

Mr Donald Barnes

Headmaster from 29 May 1933 until retiral on 5 July 1968

New unit for P1-P3 children from Ballingry opened on present site on 30 August 1957; officially opened on 13 December 1957, when "the building was handed over to Mr Sneddon, Convener of Fife County Council by Provost Playfair, Vice-Chairman of the Education Committee".

New building for remainder of school on present site officially opened by Councillor Norman Graham on 12 November 1965.

Mr A. Raymond

Headmaster from 30 August 1968 until retiral in August 1978

Mrs M. Aitken

Headteacher from August 1978 until retiral in May 1986

Mrs K. Dewar

Headteacher from May 1986 to present

CROSSHILL SCHOOL

Extract from log of Ballingry Public School Infant Department for 7 February 1927: "Ballingry Crosshill Infant School was destroyed by fire on Wednesday night 26th January. Consequently the children are coming to Ballingry Public School since Monday 31st".

Oldest surviving log records opening on 4 February 1929, with an Opening Ceremony at 4 pm, conducted by Rev. Mr Scanlan of Strathmiglo, member of the Education Authority.

Mr A. Stuart
Headmaster from day of opening until his sudden death on 14 June 1944

Mr James V. Bayne
Headmaster from 1 September 1944 to summer 1949

Mr James Hood
Headmaster from 29 August 1949 until his death on 26 December 1965

Miss Page
Interim Headteacher, January to May 1966

Mr E. R. Brook
Headmaster from 16 May 1966 until appointed Headmaster of Kennoway on 3 October 1969.

Mr John Brown
Headmaster from 2 February 1970 until appointed Headmaster of Aberhill on 1 February 1974

Mrs Robertson
Acting Headteacher, February to April 1974

Mrs Agnes Ritchie
Headteacher from 15 April 1974 until appointed Headteacher of Methilhill on 28 April 1980

Mrs Ferguson
Acting Headteacher, April to August 1980

Mr David Paterson
Headteacher from 18 August 1980 until appointed Headteacher of Dunnikier on 2 February 1986

Mr James Greig
Headteacher from 14 April 1986 until closure of school, when appointed Headteacher of St Leonards

School closed December 1989, when pupils transferred to new Benarty Primary School.

BENARTY PRIMARY SCHOOL

School opened at 9 a.m. on 28 August 1950, when Mr David Martin OBE introduced headteacher to staff. 584 pupils on roll.

Mr Robert Nisbet
Headteacher from 29 August 1950 until appointed Headteacher of Dunnikier on 30 April 1986

Mr James Mailer
Headteacher from 1 May 1956 until his death on 8 January 1962

Mr William Halyburton
Interim Headteacher, February to April 1962

Mr A. P. King
Headteacher from 16 April 1962 until appointed Headteacher of Langlands on 29 March 1968

Mr J. M. Brook
Headteacher from 26 August 1968 until retiral on 29 June 1979

Mrs E. Adrain
Headteacher from 22 October 1979 until appointed Headteacher of Camdean on 2 July 1982

Mrs A. Hutton
Acting Headteacher August to December 1982

Mrs R. Hughes
Headteacher from 6 January 1983 until appointed Primary Adviser, Central Region, 30 September 1990

Miss A. Howitt
Headteacher from 7 January 1991 to present

Ballingry School

St Kenneth's School, Crosshill

Fife County and Regional Councillors 1932—1992

BALLINGRY

David Martin — Elected December 1932 — Retired 1952 — Died 21.05.73
Mrs Margaret Blair — Elected — 27th May, 1952 — Re-elected 1955
Lawrence Daly — Elected May 1958 — Re-elected May 1961
Patrick Kelly — Elected May 1964 — Retired May 1967
Norman Graham — Elected May 1967 — Re-elected May 1970
William Clarke — Elected May 1973

BALLINGRY SOUTH

Alexander Moffat — Elected December 1932 — Resigned 24th May, 1945
Robert Smith — Elected 26th June, 1945
Patrick Kelly — Elected 17th May, 1949

BALLINGRY CENTRAL (Changed to Crosshill)

Alex Page — Elected December 1932 — December 1938
W. Marshall — Elected December 1938 — Resigned 4th December, 1946
Norman Graham — Elected 28th January, 1947 — Returned May 1949/52/55/58/61/64

CROSSHILL (Formerly Ballingry Central) (Changed to Ballingry 1967)

Norman Graham — Elected May 1955 — Re-elected May 1958, May 1961, May 1964
Samuel McPherson — Elected May 1967 — Re-elected 1970/73

LOCHORE

James Robertson — Elected 1952
Thomas Thomson — Elected May 1955 — Re-elected 1958/61/64
Resigned 1967 (Killed in road accident 19.11.74)
Angelo Valente — Elected May 1967 — Re-elected 1970/1973

LUMPHINNANS

P. J. Kelly — Elected May 1952 — 1955
Robert Smith — Elected May 1955 — Re-elected May 1958/1961/1964 — Re-elected 1967/1970/1973

Printed by Barr Printers Glenrothes Limited, Poplar Road, Woodside Estate, Glenrothes, Fife KY7 4AA.
Telephone: (0592) 753763   Fax: (0592) 755043